100 *Belgian Icons*

100
Belgian
Icons **Derek Blyth**

LUSTER

TABLE OF CONTENTS

INTRODUCTION

Belgium is a curious country. Maybe the strangest country in the world. It is the birthplace of Magritte, Tintin and The Singing Nun. It is also the country that invented the saxophone, pigeon racing and art nouveau architecture. Its people are passionate about cycle racing, eating fries with mayonnaise and vertical archery. It has the world's best bar, brews the world's best beer and grows the world's most expensive vegetable. Yet people say Belgium is boring. How can everyone be so wrong?

The answer could be that no one really knows Belgium. Not even the people who live there. Every journey is an adventure into the unknown, even if it is just a few kilometres down the road. You never know what you are going to come across – a forgotten battlefield, a procession of giants or a bridge going nowhere.

People often have trouble defining Belgium, but this small country does have its own distinctive identity. It is definitely not France, although French is the language of southern Belgium. It is not the Netherlands, although more than half the population speak Dutch. And it could never be mistaken for Germany, despite a small enclave of German speakers in East Belgium. It is *Belgium*. But what does that mean, exactly?

This book tries to make sense of the country by describing 100 icons that make Belgium different from anywhere else. It is about the music they play, the sauce they order with their fries, the curious things they do at the coast.

It begins with food, because anyone who thinks of Belgium thinks of beer, chocolate and fries. And that makes sense. Belgium is a land where people take food seriously. Maybe too seriously. Sometimes they talk of nothing else. Everyone will have an opinion on the best place at the coast for *moules-frites,* or the correct beer to drink in a Liège bar, or the obscure chocolate shop in Bruges that is so much better than the ones the tourists visit.

This book is also about the curious national obsessions that are typically Belgian, like front gardens, cobbled roads and Expo 58 souvenirs. It is about parades of giants, the language border and the curious history of the national anthem.

People often dismiss Belgium as unimportant. Even Belgians can be surprisingly critical of their country. Maybe they are right. Belgium is a small country on the edge of Europe. It doesn't pretend to be important. And yet. It might be that you just have to look in the right places to discover that this country is actually quite cool, quirky and different, in 100 different ways.

THE AUTHOR

Derek Blyth has lived in Belgium for 30 years. Long enough to know that Belgium is complicated. As a travel journalist, he has visited almost every corner of the country. He has tried rare beers, eaten in remote Ardennes restaurants, walked the Belgian coast. He has tried every possible way to understand the country.

A former editor of *The Bulletin* magazine and *Flanders Today* newspaper, he has written countless articles to explain Belgium, along with a bestselling travel guide to *The 500 Hidden Secrets of Brussels*, along with similar guides to Antwerp, Ghent, Bruges and Belgium. He also organises walking tours in Belgian cities and blogs about odd details of life in Belgium and the Netherlands.

THE ILLUSTRATOR

Emma Verhagen is an architecture student at Sint-Lucas Ghent. When asked to illustrate this book, she decided to capture the identity of Belgium in 100 miniature images, ranging from a portion of fries to the Belgian coast.

ICONIC
pleasures

Frietmuseum
Vlamingstraat 33
Bruges
+32 (0)50 34 01 50
frietmuseum.be

FRIES

Let's be clear about one thing. You don't call them French fries. They are *frietjes*, or *frites*, or fries if you insist. But certainly not French fries. Not in Belgium anyway.

No one is absolutely certain who invented the fried potato. The Belgian historian Jo Gérard has argued it all began in Wallonia in the 1680s during a cold winter. With the rivers frozen, the locals had no fish to eat, so they fried potatoes in oil. Maybe that is how it started. Or maybe it began in Spain.

The concept of 'French' fries emerged during the First World War when British and American soldiers discovered fried potatoes in Flanders. As French was the official language in Belgium at the time, the soldiers assumed they were in France eating French fries.

It makes sense. But the main reason Belgians hate the name French fries is that French fries are quite different from Belgian fries. The proper Belgian fried potato is prepared with enormous patience and skill. The correct potato must be used. The Bintje if it is in season. Or the Allegria, or something similar. It should be peeled by hand and sliced into the correct size. Then it is fried once in beef dripping at 160°C, laid aside until cool, and fried a second time at 180°C.

And it's not done yet. This is slow fast food. So the fries are scooped out of the bubbling fat, dropped into a large metal sieve, and shaken to remove the excess fat. They are then scooped into a paper cone, but not all at once. The correct method is to serve a small portion, add a dash of salt, add some more fries, more salt, and so on. It takes time, but the fries you finally get are perfect – soft on the inside and crisp on the outside.

Then you just need to choose a sauce from the long list of options. You might go for the classic mayonnaise. Or something with a kick, like Samurai, or Pikanto or Mexicano. Or even the fiery Lucifer sauce if you are up for a challenge.

Neuhaus
Galerie de la Reine 25-27
Brussels
+32 (0)2 568 23 00
neuhauschocolates.com

Chocoladehuis Boon
Paardsdemerstraat 13
Hasselt
+32 (0)11 42 21 99
chocoladehuisboon.be

CHOCOLATE

Anyone who travels to Belgium is told to bring back some Belgian chocolates. This small country might be obscure, but everyone knows about its chocolates.

The history of chocolate making in Belgium goes back to the 18th century when the aristocracy developed a taste for hot chocolate. The business grew in scale in the 19th century when cocoa beans were imported from Congo.

The Belgian industry really took off in 1912 when pharmacist Jean Neuhaus invented the *praline*. It involved a thin chocolate mould with a sweet, creamy filling. Neuhaus sold his chocolates among his cough syrups in a beautiful gilded shop in the Galerie de la Reine in Brussels. His wife Louise added her own creative touch by designing the folding *ballotin* box. The original shop is still there, minus the medicines.

The large Belgian producers like Neuhaus and Godiva are now global brands owned by giant multinationals. The chocolates are still good, but there's something missing. For an authentic chocolate experience, you need to visit one of the small family-run businesses. You find them in most Belgian towns, sometimes hidden down a quiet side street, like Frederic Blondeel in the Brussels suburb of Koekelberg, or Boon in Hasselt.

The chocolates are often handmade in small batches in a workshop at the back of the shop. They might be based on secret recipes that have been handed down through the generations. The finished chocolates are laid out on trays to let customers pick their favourites. Most people buy 250 or 300 grams. Not too much, because proper chocolates have to be eaten within a week or ten days. All this takes time. It is a craft.

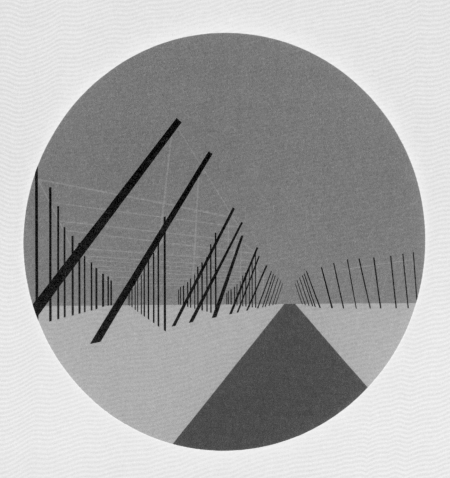

Hopmuseum
Gasthuisstraat 71
Poperinge
+32 (0)57 33 79 22
hopmuseum.be

Restaurant 't Hommelhof
Watouplein 17
Watou
+32 (0)57 38 80 24
hommelhof.be

HOP SHOOTS

You occasionally see hop shoots on the menu in Belgian restaurants. But not often, because hop shoots have a short season of two months and sell for prices that can make them the most expensive vegetables in the world. Local farmers aren't kidding when they talk about 'polder gold'.

The *hoppescheuten* are mainly cultivated in the region around Poperinge in West Flanders. They are gathered by cutting the tiny white shoots from the roots of hop plants. The work has to be done in the dead of winter when the weather is often cold and wet. It is hardly surprising that early shoots can sell at auction for as much as 1000 euro a kilo, compared with a couple of euros for a kilo of potatoes.

The shoots appear on restaurant menus from about mid-February until late March. They have a unique bitter taste that is fresh and grassy. Poached in water, the shoots are served in trendy restaurants, along with North Sea grey shrimps or perhaps Ostend oysters.

The restaurant 't Hommelhof in Watou offers a creative menu every year that uses local hops in every course, while the Hop Museum in Poperinge organises a hop shoot festival in March involving workshops, tastings and bike tours of the hop fields.

De Hopduvel
Coupure Links 625
Ghent
+32 (0)9 225 20 68
dehopduivel.be

A c't'heure dînant
Rue Grande 146
Dinant
+32 (0)82 61 38 42
*actheuredinant.
wordpress.com*

BEER

They have been brewing beer in Belgium since the Middle Ages. So they know how to do it. Some of the finest beers in the world are brewed by Trappist monks in six ancient abbeys deep in the countryside. Other exceptional beers are created in village breweries that only produce enough to supply the local cafe.

The Belgians take beer drinking very seriously. Almost every beer in the land has its own shape of glass, which means cafes have to keep an enormous supply of glasses. Some Trappist beer glasses look as if they are designed for a church service, while Pauwel Kwak beers are served in a hunting glass with a round base and its own wooden support.

This small country produces an astonishing number of beers. One Belgian beer book lists 1500 different varieties. They range in style from the sour Lambics of the Zenne valley near Brussels to the unique red beers of West Flanders, which are fermented by rare bacteria.

There was a time when the beer culture of Belgium seemed to be dying out. By the early 20th century, Brussels was down to one brewery producing a sour Gueuze almost no one drank. But then Belgian beers became trendy in other countries. The British, Dutch and Americans developed a taste for distinctive Belgian beers. And finally Belgians have started to appreciate their rich beer heritage.

Belgium is now Europe's biggest exporter of beers, according to the Brewers of Europe federation, with 17,5 million hectolitres leaving the country every year.

Many old breweries have been rescued, while small-scale craft projects have started up in abandoned industrial spaces. More than ten small breweries have sprung up in Brussels in recent years, including a cluster in the Dansaert district, where a beer museum is planned to open in 2023 in the old stock exchange.

MUSSELS

The Belgians have a strange love affair with mussels. They like to order large iron pots filled with shiny black-shelled mussels. Traditionally, they are eaten at the coast in restaurants like Kombuis in Ostend and Oesterput in Blankenberge. But you can also order a pot at Chez Léon in Brussels, where they have been serving mussels since 1893.

Eating mussels is a Belgian ritual. The empty shell is used like tweezers to prise the soft mussel from its shell. The empty shells are deposited in a large bowl that soon fills to the brim.

The mussels are cooked in various ways. The popular *moules marinière* are simmered in a briny broth of chopped celery, onions, parsley and white wine. They are served with a large bowl of fries, a jar of Hollandaise sauce, a pot of mayonnaise and a wipe to clean your hands once the last mussel has been fished out of the brine.

The odd thing is that the mussels they eat in Belgium are mostly raised along the Dutch coast in fishing towns like Yerseke in Zeeland. The Dutch don't share the Belgian love of molluscs, so most of the harvest is shipped off to Brussels, Ostend and Antwerp.

It used to be you could only eat fresh mussels in months with an 'r' in the word. That meant the season ran from September to April. But mussels are now frozen which allows restaurants to serve them all year.

There is always something for Belgians to complain about. Some years the mussels are too small. Some years they arrive late because of bad weather. And the price seems to go up every year. But Belgians still eat them, no matter what.

BROODJE MARTINO

Most sandwiches in Belgium are ordinary. But the Martino is surprising. Some say it was invented by a professional footballer called Albert De Hert who ran a snack bar on the De Coninckplein in Antwerp. One day in 1951, a footballer called Theo Maertens came into the snack bar looking for something to eat. His nickname was Martino. He was a little drunk and asked Albert to make him up a sandwich that included everything that he had in the cool cabinet.

Albert got to work. He sliced a baguette, spread it with raw steak américain, then added chopped onion, sliced gherkin, pili-pili sauce, cayenne pepper, ketchup, Worcester sauce and a dash of Tabasco. The *broodje Martino* was born.

Or maybe not. A snack bar in Ghent called Martino claims it invented the sandwich during the Second World War. A hungry German soldier went into Martino and asked for the best sandwich on the menu. He was served a sandwich with raw mince, along with onions, egg, anchovies and Tabasco sauce. It was meant to be disgusting, an act of defiance, but the German loved it.

No one knows the true story. But the Martino snack bar in Ghent stopped serving the Martino in 2007. It was just too much trouble, the owner said.

NEUZEKES

It started in 2011 on the pretty Groentenmarkt in Ghent. A trader had set up a wooden cart in the square piled high with the popular local sweets known as *neuzekes*. The move annoyed Carl Demeestere, who sold the sweets in his shop. He retaliated by setting up his own stand nearby, leading to a bitter commercial rivalry that lasted almost a decade, involving insults, fights, court cases, a temporary trading ban and finally, in 2019, a 30-metre exclusion zone.

At the heart of the dispute is a strange conical sweet with a sticky raspberry filling and hard outer shell. It was invented in the late 19th century, possibly by a priest in Bruges, or, more likely, a Ghent pharmacist called De Vick who accidentally left some cough syrup until it had developed a hard crust. Because of the distinctive shape, the sweets became known in Flanders as *neuzekes*, or little noses.

Down south in Wallonia, they are called *cuberdons*, possibly from the term *bonnet de curé* – a priest's hat. Or it might come from the rude term *cul de bourdon* – literally, a bee's arse, but slang for a woman's shapely bottom.

The exact recipe is a closely guarded secret known only to a few producers. The main ingredient is raspberry which gives the filling its dark crimson colour. The recipe also involves sugar, gelatin and gum Arabic collected from the sap of acacia trees in the Sahel region of Africa. Ideally, like pralines, they should be eaten within a few weeks.

Belgians are deeply fond of these delicious sweets with their sweet syrup. They enjoy the ritual of biting off the tip, then sucking up the syrup. It takes some skill to avoid it dripping onto your clothes.

For many Belgians, the *cuberdon* is a taste of childhood. Even if it has led to a war in the heart of Ghent.

Himschoot Bakkerij
Groentenmarkt 1
Ghent
+32 (0)491 52 83 31
bakkerijhimschoot.be

Bakkerij Goossens
Korte Gasthuisstraat 31
Antwerp
+32 (0)3 226 07 91

CRAMIQUE

One thing Belgium does well is comfort food. Maybe it's because of the miserable winters. But you get really tasty food that leaves you feeling good. You can boost your spirits on a rainy Sunday morning just by visiting a local bakery and picking up something for breakfast, like croissants or *pains au chocolat*. Or you can go for the full Belgian experience and buy a *cramique* loaf still warm from the oven.

Known as *rozijnenbrood* in Flanders, *cramique* is a light, sweet brioche-style raisin bread. Some bakers offer a more sophisticated version known as *suikerbrood* in Flanders, which is filled with small lumps of sugar. Hence the name *craquelin*, or crackling, in French-speaking Wallonia and Brussels.

Belgians used to wait in line to pick up *cramique* at the local baker. It would be a social occasion when you could catch up on family news and local gossip. But many local bakeries have closed down in recent years, leaving just a few traditional bakers like Himschoot in Ghent, with its dark-green façade, warm aroma and wooden shelves lined with different types of loaves.

Or there is Bakkerij Goossens in Antwerp where the Goossens family have been baking bread since 1884. The owners still roll and knead the dough in the same little shop where the business began. There is hardly space for more than two people inside, but locals don't mind waiting outside in the rain to pick up their daily bread.

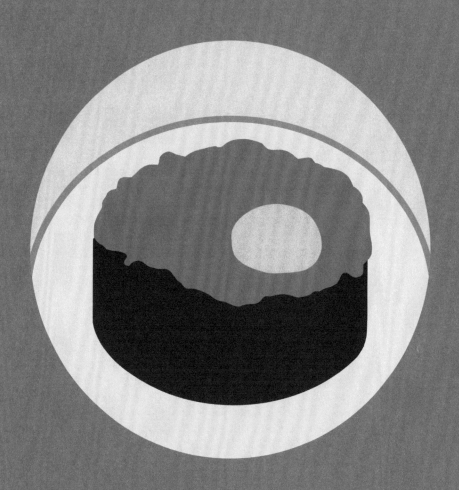

Au Vieux Saint Martin
Place du Grand Sablon 38
Brussels
+32 (0)2 512 64 76
auvieuxsaintmartin.be

Friture René
Place de la Résistance 14
Anderlecht
+32 (0)2 523 28 76

STEAK AMÉRICAIN

It's easy to make a mistake when you see *steak américain* on the restaurant menu. You might order it thinking you will be served a plump, juicy beefsteak like they serve in American diners. And you are probably going to be disappointed when it turns out to be raw mince.

But this Belgian speciality is a lot more than just raw mince. It is composed of the best chopped beef bound with raw egg yolks, and flavoured with mayonnaise, piccalilli, finely chopped onions, capers, parsley and a dash of Lea & Perrins Worcestershire sauce. Served with proper Belgian fries.

The original recipe was created in 1926 by Joseph Niels in his elegant hotel restaurant Canterbury down in the centre of Brussels. He based it on the traditional French dish *steak tartare,* which had become popular in Belgium in the 1920s. But he was fed up serving steak tartare and invented his own version in 1926, adding a dash of Worcestershire sauce.

It was a time when Belgians were fascinated by all aspects of American culture, from jazz to skyscrapers, so the new dish was given the exotic name *steak américain.* It quickly became a Belgian classic served in brasseries and restaurants.

The original restaurant Canterbury has closed down, but Joseph's son Albert put the dish on the menu when he opened his restaurant Au Vieux Saint Martin in 1968. This stylish 1960s restaurant in the heart of the antique district is still one of the best places to order the dish, if you dare.

Estaminet
De Peerdevisscher
Pastoor Schmitzstraat 4
Oostduinkerke
+32 (0)58 51 32 57

't Werftje
Werfkaai 29
Zeebrugge
+32 (0)497 55 30 10
twerftje.be

SHRIMP CROQUETTES

The Belgian coast has several local specialities you definitely need to try. Mussels of course. And Ostend sole. But also croquettes made with tiny North Sea shrimps.

The grey shrimps are caught every morning in the fishing towns along the coast. In Oostduinkerke, a group of local fishermen ride enormous horses into the waves every morning to trawl the shallow water for shrimps.

Almost every traditional Belgian restaurant along the coast serves *garnaalkroketten (croquettes de crevettes* in French). They are served at lunch fresh from the sea, along with a slice of lemon and a sprig of deep-fried parsley.

Everyone has their own opinion about the best place on the coast for shrimp croquettes. It might be an elegant seafront brasserie in Knokke, or a simple bar on the Nieuwpoort harbour front.

The Estaminet De Peerdevisscher in Oostduinkerke, next to the national fishing museum NAVIGO, is run by a former shrimp fisherman who used to ride his horse into the sea. So he knows where to get the freshest catch.

But maybe 't Werftje on the old harbour in Zeebrugge is the most authentic spot to try the local speciality. The wood-panelled interior is decorated with nostalgic fishing photos, ship parts and an old iron stove.

WITLOOF

A mysterious vegetable known as *witloof* is cultivated in dark farmhouse cellars around Brussels and Leuven. It is a pure Belgian creation that was originally cultivated by the horticulturist Frans Breziers in the Brussels Botanical Garden. He spent the winter of 1850-51 growing chicory in old cellars used for mushroom cultivation. Covered by a layer of warm, dark horse manure, the chicory emerged as a pale, slightly yellow vegetable.

Local farmers learned of the technique and started to grow *witloof* in the fertile soil of Flemish Brabant, east of Brussels. The bitter, white vegetable took a few years to catch on, first in Brussels and then in Paris.

The name varies depending on where you buy it. They call it *witloof*, or white leaf, in Flanders, *chicon* in Wallonia, and *endive* in France. The Italian name is *insalata Belga*, Belgian salad, while Germans refer to it as *chicorée*. The British use the word chicory, while American cookbooks call it endive.

Known as 'white gold' in Belgium, *witloof* is still cultivated on hundreds of small farms around Brussels. It is widely used to make soups, salads and cooked dishes. The most popular preparation is *chicons au gratin,* or *witloof met ham in de oven,* a tasty oven dish made from *witloof* wrapped in ham and Béchamel sauce.

Tierenteyn-Verlent
Groentenmarkt 3
Ghent
+32 (0)9 225 83 36
tierenteyn-verlent.be

TIERENTEYN MUSTARD

You could easily miss the little green-fronted shop in the corner of Ghent's Groentenmarkt square. It has been there since 1867 selling a potent local mustard made according to a secret recipe.

Tierenteyn-Verlent is one of the oldest surviving family businesses in the country, although it is no longer run by the family that founded it. The current owners still prepare the mustard down in the ancient cellar where they grind white mustard seeds by hand and add the secret mix of ingredients that give it a special kick.

The mustard is sold in an authentic 19th-century store interior furnished with wooden shelves, old cabinets and hand-painted apothecary jars. As soon as you enter, you notice the heady aroma of herbs, tea and cinnamon.

The mustard is scooped from a wooden barrel into distinctive grey earthenware jars. Made in a small pottery works in La Roche-en-Ardenne, the jars are decorated with the Tierenteyn logo in an elegant blue rococo script.

The date on the jars – 1790 – is a little misleading, as the first mustard was produced by Petrus Tierenteyn in the early 19th century. But it is still one of the oldest businesses in the country. And the mustard recipe has hardly changed in 200 years.

Eggenols
Rue des Guillemins 92
Liège
+32 (0)4 252 28 79
eggenols.be

Wafelhuis Van Hecke
Nationalestraat 88
Antwerp
+32 (0)3 233 19 72
hof.be

WAFFLES

The smell of waffles hits you the moment you step off a train in Belgium. Freshly cooked on steaming black waffle irons, these sweet, sticky waffles are classic Belgian winter snacks. They are often sold out of the side of a bright yellow Volkswagen van that switches to selling ice cream in the summer.

The Belgian waffle was popularised at Expo 58 when Walter Cleyman set up a stand equipped with several gas-powered waffle irons. He dusted the waffles with icing sugar and served them with whipped cream and fresh fruit. They were a phenomenal success. More than 400.000 waffles were sold.

The Brussels couple Maurice and Rose Vermersch and their daughter Marie-Paule launched the concept in New York at the 1964 World Fair. They set up a waffle stand in the popular mediaeval Belgian village where they served traditional waffles made with Rose's secret batter recipe. Long queues waited patiently as the family worked furiously to make about 2500 waffles a day, sold for 99 cents. They were originally called Brussels Waffles, but the Vermersch family had to change the name to 'Bel-Gem Waffles' when they realised most Americans had never heard of Brussels.

The Walloon city of Liège has its own waffle called the *gaufre liégeoise*. This hot, sticky waffle is stuffed with sugar that caramelises during cooking. Served in thin greaseproof paper, they make the perfect comfort food to eat as you walk through the Liège streets on a winter afternoon.

Most of the waffles sold in Brussels are not Brussels waffles or Belgian waffles. They are actually sweet, sticky Liège waffles, which are easier to hold in your hand.

Nüetnigenough
Rue du Lombard 25
Brussels
+32 (0)2 513 78 84
nuetnigenough.be

STOEMP

Most Belgians have a favourite recipe for *stoemp*. Often it is handed down from a grandmother. Or it might depend on what is growing out in the back garden. It is all about something warm and comforting during the Belgian winter.

Stoemp is a dish that goes back to the 17th century. It originated in the earthy tradition of peasant cooking where you toss whatever you have dug out of the ground into one big cooking pot.

The basic ingredient is potatoes. You then add any winter vegetable you can find. It could be carrots, Brussels sprouts, onions, endives, leeks, celery or cabbage. Then you mash it all up, add a little milk or cream, some butter, and perhaps a dash of nutmeg. Served with sausage or meatballs, and a Belgian beer, it is the perfect way to get through a rainy day in January.

Stoemp eventually became unfashionable. You hardly ever found it on a restaurant menu. But then TV chef Albert Verdeyen decided to revive this old Belgian favourite. He wrote several *stoemp* cookbooks and joined with other chefs in 2017 to set up the Order of the Stoemp. You can find it in a lot more places now, including the friendly little restaurant Nüetnigenough in the heart of Brussels.

ICONIC
people

Fondation Brel
Place de la Vieille Halle
aux Blés 11
Brussels
+32 (0)2 511 10 20
fondationbrel.be

JACQUES BREL

Jacques Brel was a Belgian singer and songwriter who began his career in the 1950s in smoky dives in the centre of Brussels. He sang poetic, melancholy songs about love, death and despair that gained him a huge following in Paris. Most people thought he was French. But Brel was born in 1929 in the Brussels suburb of Schaerbeek. The first Tintin comic came out in the same year.

Jacques worked for a time in his father's cardboard box factory, before moving to Paris in 1954. Holed up in a dilapidated Paris hotel, he scratched a living for several years before he finally made a breakthrough in 1957 with his plaintive chanson *Quand on n'a que l'amour* (If we only have love). Then came *Ne me quitte pas* (If you go away), a desperate love song directed at his mistress.

Brel's performances had an extraordinary intensity as if his life depended on the song. He would sweat and spit on the stage. You can see him at his best in a live recording of his song *Amsterdam* at the Olympia in Paris in 1964.

It all came to an end, suddenly and unexpectedly, in 1966 when he performed for the last time at the Olympia. His fans begged him to stay, shouting *"Ne me quitte pas"*. But he was gone.

Brel sailed off to the Marquesas Islands in the Pacific with his mistress called Maddly Bamy. He fell ill with lung cancer, returned to Paris for treatment and died in 1978 in a Paris hospital.

In 2017, the Brussels sculptor Tom Frantzen created a bronze statue of the singer. It stands outside the Fondation Brel in Brussels run by his daughter France and her passionate little team. She has lovingly preserved a collection of recordings, photographs and family mementoes.

The Fondation Brel has also created an audio guide you can use to wander through the streets of Brussels, while listening to Brel's songs. It takes you to the places where he first found his voice.

AUDREY HEPBURN

No one can quite believe the plaque attached to a town house in a Brussels backstreet. It states that Audrey Hepburn was born at this address on 4 May 1929. She went on to become one of the world's most glamorous screen stars, as well as a style icon. But she spent her first five years in this gloomy Brussels street.

She was born Edda Kathleen Ruston. Her English father Joseph Ruston was director of the Brussels branch of the Bank of England. Her Dutch mother Ella van Heemstra was a baroness. After her parents divorced in 1935, Edda was sent to boarding school in England. She spent the war years in the Netherlands, where she suffered malnutrition during the winter of 1944-45.

Audrey Hepburn returned to Brussels as UNICEF ambassador in 1992, just a few months before she died. She gave an interview in perfect Dutch in which she remembered the delicious Belgian chocolate from her childhood.

ANNE TERESA DE KEERSMAEKER

No one thinks of Brussels as a dance capital. It's known for EU politics, waffles and chocolate, not contemporary dance. Yet this city has nurtured some of the world's most talented choreographers and dancers.

It took off in 1960 when Swiss choreographer Maurice Béjart founded his Ballet du XX Siècle and dance school Mudra in Brussels. Based in the Monnaie opera house, Béjart brought astonishing modern ballet productions to the conservative Belgian capital.

A new wave of dance emerged in the 1980s under Belgian choreographer Anne Teresa De Keersmaeker. Born in Mechelen in 1960, she studied at Mudra under Béjart before creating a series of avant-garde works that combined strict minimalism with hypnotic rhythms. De Keersmaeker went on to set up Rosas dance company and P.A.R.T.S. dance school in an old industrial district close to Brussels Midi station.

De Keersmaeker is now one of the world's most inspiring choreographers. You can track down some of her works on internet sites. Her 1983 feminist work *Rosas danst Rosas* remains a key milestone of modern dance, while the sublime 2001 work *Rain* combines hypnotic dance with Steven Reich's pulsating music.

De Keersmaeker shows no sign of slowing down. In 2020, she worked in New York with Belgian theatre director Ivo van Hove on a radical new stage version of the Broadway musical *West Side Story.*

Liège tourist office
AT: Halle aux Viandes
Quai de la Goffe 13
Liège
+32 (0)4 221 92 21
visitezliege.be

GEORGES SIMENON

Most people think the writer Georges Simenon was French, but he was born in Liège in 1903. He moved to Paris when he was 20, and set most of his books in France, so there is a reason for the confusion.

The young Simenon spent his early years in the rainy industrial city on the edge of the Ardennes. He grew up in the Outremeuse district and left school at 16 to work as a journalist on a local newspaper.

Simenon wrote hundreds of books, mostly bleak crime fiction sold at railway stations, but also serious novels and autobiography. His characters were ordinary people living grim lives as concierges, waiters or shopkeepers, until something bad happens to them. His most famous character was Inspector Jules Maigret, the grumpy Paris detective who seemed more Belgian than French, with his pipe and bowler hat, his little routines and his sympathy for the underdog.

Simenon was an astonishingly prolific writer. By the end of his life, he had written 400 books, including 103 Maigret novels and more than 100 serious novels. Go into any secondhand bookshop, anywhere in the world, and you will find some forgotten little book by Simenon. Take it to read on the train. You will not be disappointed. When the French novelist André Gide was asked which of Simenon's books one should read first, he replied: "All of them!"

It is essential to visit Liège if you want to understand Simenon's world. The tourist office has created a booklet to guide you around the spots linked to Simenon, including the apartment building where he was born on Friday 13 February (his superstitious mother lied about the date), the war memorial outside the town hall with the name Maigret on it, and the narrow alleys of the old town.

Diane von Fürstenberg
store
Rue du Grand Cerf 11
Brussels
+32 (0)2 648 62 24
dvf.com

DIANE VON FÜRSTENBERG

She spent most of her career in New York and Paris, but Diane von Fürstenberg grew up in Brussels. Her Jewish father migrated to Belgium from Moldova in 1929. Her Greek mother had been held in Auschwitz concentration camp during the war. Diane was born in 1946.

After a comfortable Belgian childhood, Diane was sent to boarding schools in Switzerland and England. She then studied textile design in Italy and began designing women's clothes soon after her marriage to German aristocrat Prince Egon von Fürstenberg. "I had to be someone of my own, and not just a plain little girl who got married beyond her desserts," she explained.

After moving to New York, Von Fürstenberg created her famous knitted jersey wrap dress in 1974. Based on a skirt combined with a wrap top, it was printed with patterns inspired by Andy Warhol's pop art. Her business rapidly expanded, and Von Fürstenberg went on to create cosmetics and a perfume, as well as setting up several charities.

The iconic wrap dress has become a timeless classic worn by celebrities such as Michelle Obama, Madonna and Kate Middleton. It was the focus of a large-scale exhibition in 2009 titled *Diane von Fürstenberg: Journey of a Dress*.

Von Fürstenberg has been listed as one of the world's 100 most powerful women, as well as one of the 50 most influential Jews. At the age of 71, she returned to her birthplace to receive the title of honorary citizen of the city of Brussels.

STROMAE

His father was from Rwanda, his mother is Flemish, and he sings in French. You might describe Stromae as a typical Belgian mix. His real name is Paul Van Haver, but he performs as Stromae. The name comes from 'Maestro' with the syllables reversed.

Stromae began to get noticed in 2010 when he released a catchy song in French titled *Alors on danse* (So We Dance). Its bitter lyrics on themes like divorce and debt captured the desolate mood of Europe in the grip of economic crisis. The song became a No. 1 hit in 12 European countries. The video clip has been viewed more than two hundred million times on YouTube.

Stromae made another clip on a miserable rainy morning in Brussels in 2013, when he pretended to stagger around drunk on the busy Place Louise as he sang the song *Formidable* (Wonderful). The video posted on YouTube became another viral hit.

As well as recording a string of hit songs, Van Haver has emerged as a Belgian fashion icon with his fondness for bright cardigans, bow ties and stylish shoes. He likes to squeeze his tall body into a tiny yellow Fiat 500 to complete the impeccable image, which he describes as a bridge between English style and African dandyism.

Some people say he is the new Jacques Brel. Others argue he is one of the few people who can hold Belgium together. But maybe Stromae would just prefer to be known as the maestro.

Modemuseum Hasselt
Gasthuisstraat 11
Hasselt
+32 (0)11 23 96 21
modemuseumhasselt.be

MoMu
Nationalestraat 28
Antwerp
momu.be

THE ANTWERP SIX

It started with a rented van. In 1986, six Antwerp fashion graduates drove a van filled with clothes from Belgium to Britain to show off their designs at London Fashion Week. They caused a sensation. Everyone loved the cool, melancholy Antwerp style after the glitzy excesses of the early 1980s.

The only problem was their names – Marina Yee, Dries Van Noten, Ann Demeulemeester, Walter Van Beirendonck, Dirk Bikkembergs and Dirk Van Saene. No one could pronounce them and so a London journalist came up with a neat solution. He called them the 'Antwerp Six', as if they were bank robbers on the run or terrorists who had just set off a bomb in Central London.

The Antwerp Six put an end to the old joke about boring Belgium. Here were six of the most creative people in Europe. Dries Van Noten opened his first tiny boutique in Antwerp the following year, Walter Van Beirendonck displayed his wild clothes in an abandoned garage, and Ann Demeulemeester launched a stylishly minimalist store dedicated to her darkly goth style.

Fashionistas began to visit Antwerp to savour the radical fashion style. A new luxury industry emerged that spread to Brussels, Hasselt and Liège. A fashion museum opened in Hasselt in 1986, followed in 2002 by the spectacular MoMu in the heart of Antwerp's fashion district. The big international fashion houses began to recruit a new wave of Belgians trained at the Antwerp Academy, including Olivier Theyskens, Raf Simons and Kris Van Assche. The Antwerp Six had made Belgium cool.

THE SINGING NUN

It sounds like an urban myth, but in 1963 a singing nun from Belgium beat the Beatles to the top of the U.S. charts. She went on to scandalise the Catholic Church with a song in praise of contraception and finally committed suicide with her lesbian lover.

Jeannine Deckers was born in 1933 in the Brussels suburb of Laeken where her father owned a patisserie shop. She joined the Girl Scouts and in 1959 withdrew into a Dominican convent near Waterloo in defiance of her strict parents.

A talented singer and guitar player, Deckers performed under the stage name 'Sœur Sourire' (Sister Smile). She became unexpectedly famous in 1963 when her song *Dominique*, dedicated to the founder of the Dominican order, became a global hit.

Three years later, Debbie Reynolds starred in the film *The Singing Nun,* based on Decker's life. Since then, the English version of *Dominique* has turned up in several films and TV series, as well as in an episode of *The Simpsons.*

But the story ended in tragedy. Deckers left the convent in 1966 after she fell out with the nuns. One year later, she caused outrage among her Catholic fans when she released a song in support of contraception titled *Glory be to God for the Golden Pill.* Pursued by the tax authorities, and haunted by guilt, she committed suicide with her female lover in 1985.

A second film on her life titled *Sœur Sourire* was made in 2009 by the Belgian director Stijn Coninx. It starred Cécile de France as the tormented nun from a Brussels suburb who enchanted the world for a few brief years.

Eddy Merckx
metro station
Anderlecht

EDDY MERCKX

Cycle racing is a Belgian obsession. This little country of cobbled roads and surprising hills is home to countless famous riders and classic races. But one name keeps coming up when you talk to Belgians about cycling. Eddy Merckx, they tell you, was the greatest Belgian cyclist. Maybe even the greatest in the world.

Born in the summer of 1945, his parents ran a grocery store in a quiet Brussels suburb. Merckx wanted to be a cyclist from the age of four and spent his summer holidays listening to Tour de France commentary on the radio. After training on race tracks in Brussels, he won his first race in 1961. Turning professional, he became known as the Cannibal because, the daughter of a rival remarked, he would eat up the competition. He won 525 races in his career, including the Tour de France five times and the Giro d'Italia five times. In one year alone, he took part in 195 races, ending the season bruised and battered. For a couple of decades in the 1960s and 1970s, he was everywhere. No one could beat him.

Merckx quit racing in 1978, but he remains a Belgian hero. He can sometimes be spotted watching Anderlecht play football, or eating *croquettes de crevettes* in his favourite Brussels restaurant. His name now appears on a Brussels school, a metro station and a square. But the best monument is his old steel-framed racing bike displayed in a glass case in Eddy Merckx metro station.

He rode the bike in 1972 when he broke the hour record in Mexico City, cycling 49,4 kilometres in one hour. For the next 12 years, no one beat the record set by the Cannibal. Yet Merckx was always modest about his achievements. He wasn't interested in fame. He just loved cycling.

THE ROYAL FAMILY

Belgians are modest. And proud of it. It's not done in Belgium to be boastful. You will be mocked if you are arrogant. Even the royal family are modest. They blend in nicely with everyone else.

King Albert II, who reigned from 1993 until he abdicated in 2013, was the least royal of the Belgian kings. He had secret affairs, an illegitimate daughter and rode a motorcycle. On Belgian national holidays, he would invite local people into the palace for drinks.

You might come across the current royal family anywhere in Belgium. The children go to a normal school in the centre of Brussels. The king and queen turn up at events like anyone else. In the summer, the royal palace in Brussels is open to everyone and the royal greenhouses can be visited for a few weeks in the spring.

You might spot the royal family sitting on a restaurant terrace in central Brussels, like any other Belgian family. No gold coach. No guards in scarlet jackets. Nothing pompous. Just an average family.

Hergé Museum
Rue du Labrador 26
Louvain-la-Neuve
+32 (0)10 48 84 21
museeherge.com

Tintin mural
Rue de l'Etuve 37
Brussels

TINTIN

He's the most famous Belgian. Everyone knows Tintin (Kuifje in Dutch). Even if you have never read a comic book in your life, you know about the smart Belgian boy with the funny hair and the white dog. Most Belgian homes have a stack of Tintin albums in an upstairs bedroom. Everyone has a favourite character, a favourite album.

Born Georges Remi in 1907, Hergé (his pen name, based on his initials, R and G, reversed) said he had an average boyhood in Brussels' rather grey Etterbeek district. He liked drawing, and discovered friendship and adventure in the Boy Scouts. His breakthrough came in 1929 when he drew his first sketchy Tintin cartoon for a Brussels newspaper. Slowly, patiently, he developed a distinctive style of storytelling.

Tintin was, in a way, the perfect Belgian. He was curious, modest and somehow always managed to defeat the bad guys. But Hergé wasn't quite so perfect. He got a little too close to the Nazis during the Second World War when he worked for *Le Soir* newspaper. His comic books sometimes reflected old colonial attitudes. He had his failings.

And yet, Hergé is still a national hero. He is celebrated in a bright, joyful museum designed by French architect Christian de Portzamparc. It is located, unexpectedly, in the new university town of Louvain-la-Neuve, a 30-minute train trip from Brussels.

Opened in 2009, the museum is a bold white design with windows that look like comic book frames. The interior incorporates a vast atrium with meandering footbridges and colourful walls inspired by Hergé's distinctive graphic style. The collection is rich in humour and odd little details, just like your favourite Tintin adventure.

EXILES

Belgium has a long history of accepting exiles, rebels and refugees. It goes back to the progressive Constitution of 1831 that protected freedom of religion, education, press and assembly.

The German philosopher Karl Marx found sanctuary in Brussels in 1845. He rented various apartments in the city, met Belgian socialists and began working on his famous *Communist Manifesto*. But finally the authorities decided he was too dangerous, and he was forced to move to London.

Belgium's tolerant climate also attracted a number of political exiles from France, among them Victor Hugo, who spent several months in Brussels in 1851 and returned here in 1861 to complete the manuscript of *Les Misérables*. The writer Alexandre Dumas also moved to Brussels in 1851, claiming he was a political exile while the real reason was to escape his creditors.

In the 1930s, the country became a safe haven for Jews fleeing Nazi Germany. Many settled in the beach town of Ostend, including the writers Stefan Zweig and Joseph Roth. The scientist Albert Einstein liked to visit the Belgian coast and stayed in the little resort of De Haan after he was banned from entering Germany in 1933. His stay is marked by a statue in a small park in De Haan.

More recently, the former Catalan president Carles Puigdemont found refuge in Belgium in 2017 after he was charged with sedition and rebellion. The Spanish government applied for his extradition, but the Belgian courts refused to allow it.

Other Spanish dissidents have also found a safe haven in Belgium, including the rapper Valtònyc from Mallorca who was accused of writing lyrics that encouraged terrorism and insulted the monarchy. The Spanish state once again failed to convince the Belgian courts. It seems Belgium still sticks to the fundamental values it set out in 1831.

THE RED DEVILS

Belgians don't like to brag about their country. There's a Flemish expression that nicely sums up their attitude. *Blij zijn met een dode mus,* it goes. It means happy with a dead sparrow, or basically happy with nothing.

You used to see this attitude in football when the national team – the Red Devils – was playing. The supporters were lukewarm as the team consistently failed to win. Not like the Dutch, who often reached the final. But Belgians didn't complain.

And then something changed in about 2010. The Red Devils stopped playing plodding, defensive football. The squad included a new generation of star players like Romelu Lukaku, Kevin De Bruyne, Eden Hazard and Vincent Kompany.

It used to be hard to spot a Belgian supporter but then they started to stand out in the crowd. They would wear jester hats in the national colours, carry red plastic tridents and paint the national flag on their cheeks.

The national team's multicultural composition helped to build support across the country's diverse ethnic communities. Both Lukaku and Kompany had Congolese backgrounds, while other players had family roots in Morocco, Mali, Spain and Kosovo. With a Spanish manager since 2016, the language problem was solved by communicating in English.

The football fever reached a peak on the night of 6 July 2018 when the Red Devils beat the World Cup favourite Brazil. The celebrations went on long into the night as the country realised it was as close as it had ever been to winning the World Cup. But they lost the next game, against France, which was perhaps a relief for a country that is basically happy with a dead sparrow.

De Bomma
Suikerrui 16
Antwerp
+32 (0)3 227 49 26
restaurantdebomma.be

**Royal Hôtel Restaurant
Bonhomme**
Rue de la Reffe 26
Remouchamps
+32 (0)4 384 40 06
hotelbonhomme.be

GRANDMOTHERS

Grandmothers have quite a cool reputation in Belgium. Mainly because of their home cooking. The classic grandmother dishes include tomato soup with meat balls, sausage and *stoemp*, rice pudding and chocolate mousse. But perhaps the most iconic dish to come out of grandmother's kitchen is Flemish stew made with dark Trappist beer, Ghent mustard and onions. Served with fries to keep everyone happy.

Many Belgian restaurants set out to provide nostalgic grand-mother cooking. It is called *op grootmoeders wijze* in Flanders, and *façon grand-mère* in French-speaking Belgium. You find those classic dishes in the restaurant De Bomma in Antwerp, in an interior decorated with old lamps and faded photographs of Belgian *bomma's* (grandmothers). Other addresses include Mémé Gusta in Ghent and the nostalgic Ardennes hotel-restaurant Bonhomme in Remouchamps.

The Belgian grandmother can also influence interior design. Young Belgians fondly furnish their apartments with vintage furniture from the 1970s, along with ornate lamps, best china soup bowls and Expo 58 souvenirs.

ICONIC
traditions

De Haan and
other resorts
Belgian coast
katrienvermeire.com

Museum of the National
Bank of Belgium
Rue de la Montagne aux
Herbes Potagères 57
Brussels
+32 (0)2 221 22 06
nbbmuseum.be

BEACH FLOWER SELLERS

No one knows how it started, but children have been selling paper flowers in the little resorts along the Belgian coast for at least one hundred years. They start by digging a hole in the sand to create their make-believe flower shops, carefully carving out a counter and a bench. Then they assemble the flowers out of colourful crepe paper bought in local craft shops. The children might add a little sign to indicate the shop is open. The grandparents are sometimes recruited to lend a hand with the family business.

But the strange thing about the flower sellers is that they don't trade flowers for money. They operate an informal beach economy based on handfuls of seashells. And the rules are strict. No mussel shells. No whelks. Only razor shells will do.

The Belgian artist Katrien Vermeire made a film in 2014 about the beach flower sellers in her home resort of De Haan. The Museum of the National Bank of Belgium acquired this beautiful work, titled *Der Kreislauf* (A Handful), in 2018. You can watch the 28-minute film in the stunning and almost unknown Belgian bank museum.

No one really knows why beach flower sellers exist on the Belgian coast and nowhere else. Some people have argued that the children are learning the basic rules of business. But Vermeire believes the flower sellers are immersed in a private, poetic world that only they understand.

Koersmuseum
Polenplein 15
Roeselare
+32 (0)51 26 24 00
koersmuseum.be

CYCLE RACING

It's tough on a bike in Belgium. Not like the Netherlands where cycling is a pleasure. The rural roads in Belgium are often paved with bumpy cobblestones. Add to that potholes, broken glass and road diversions along the way. You have to be mad to cycle in Belgium, people say.

And yet. It's Sunday morning, and you see tight packs of racing cyclists dressed in identical lycra jerseys. They flow gracefully across the flat landscape, speed down the canal towpaths, cross the bleak moors of Limburg. It's mainly in Flanders, where the flat landscape is perfect, but also along the towpaths and abandoned railway lines of Wallonia.

They might stop along the way at an old cafe to warm themselves in front of an iron stove. The walls covered with faded photographs of cycling heroes. Then it's back on the bikes. Another twenty kilometres of hard riding on rough roads before lunch.

The country is famous for cycle races like the Ronde van Vlaanderen and Liège-Bastogne-Liège. Each a test of endurance. Many of the low hills in the Flemish Ardennes have become gruelling cycling challenges, like the Oude Kwaremont, the Koppenberg and the Muur van Geraardsbergen. They might not look impressive compared to the Alps, but these cobbled slopes are punishing on a bike.

Some of the hills are protected monuments, ranked along with Bruges and the Grand-Place in Brussels. Even if they weren't, no local official would ever dare to put down asphalt.

It might seem mad, but Belgian cyclists love the rain, the hills, the cobbles.

FLOWER CARPET

Every two years, an enormous flower carpet is spread out on the cobblestones of Grand-Place in Brussels. More than 100 volunteers spend an entire day on their knees carefully placing about half a million begonias on huge plastic sheets marked out with a design.

Laid down a few days before the 15 August holiday, the carpet is a different design every year. One year, the coloured flowers were laid out to represent a Renaissance tapestry. Another year, in honour of the city's Turkish population, the carpet was modelled on a kilim.

The carpet is made entirely with begonia tuberosa grandiflora grown in the region around Ghent. Though the flower originated in the West Indies, it has been cultivated in the farmland around Ghent since the 1860s. It's the ideal plant for the Belgian climate, as it can survive wind, sun and heavy rain. Some 35 million plants are grown every year in a range of subtle colours, with about 80 percent exported abroad.

The first flower carpet was created by the Flemish landscape gardener Etienne Stautemas in his home town of Zottegem. He introduced the concept to the beautiful main square in Brussels in 1971. He has gone on to design more than 180 carpets across the world, but the most impressive is the carpet created every other year on Grand-Place.

CARNIVAL IN BINCHE

"Mas bravas que las fiestas de Bains" – more wild than carnival in Binche, goes an old Spanish saying. And every year on Mardi Gras, local men known as Gilles set out to prove that Binche can still put on one hell of a party by dressing up in costumes and dancing through the streets for hours on end.

The celebrations in Binche are modelled on a fabulous fiesta organised in 1549 by Mary of Hungary for her brother Charles V. Hundreds of Spanish grandees flocked into town dressed in Inca-inspired costumes decorated with stars and moons.

The carnival day begins each year at an ungodly 3.30 am when the Gilles are roused from bed by a drummer standing outside their front door. While the rest of the town is still asleep, the men squeeze into colourful costumes stuffed with fistfuls of straw.

The Gilles are divided into ten carnival societies with cheeky names like the Recalcitrants and the Incorruptibles. They add a sinister touch to their appearance by putting on white masks painted with waxed moustaches and green spectacles. Later in the day, they add huge hats decorated with hundreds of ostrich feathers imported from South Africa.

At the end of the afternoon, the Gilles are handed small wicker baskets filled with blood oranges. Soon there are oranges flying everywhere. They smash into the chicken wire and slam into walls leaving blood-red stains. Nowhere is *mas bravas*.

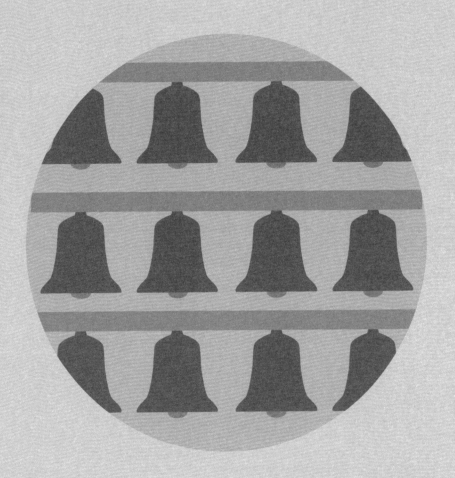

Belfry
Bruges
carillon-brugge.be

Carillon School
Bruul 52
Mechelen
beiaardschool.mechelen.be

CARILLONS

When David Bowie died in 2016, there were many tributes, but possibly the strangest ceremony happened in Bruges. The town carilloneur climbed the 366 stone steps to the top of the belfry, sat down at a keyboard, and banged out the notes of Bowie's famous song *Space Oddity*. People stopped in the street, puzzled at first, and then surprised, as the bells played the familiar melody across the old town.

Most cities in Belgium have a set of carillon bells hung in an ancient tower on the main square. They are programmed to strike the hour, the half hour, and the quarter hours. But they can also be played on an instrument that looks like a piano.

The earliest concerts were performed in 1887 by the Mechelen city carilloneur Jef Denyn. He developed an expressive way of playing that appealed to people at the time. His evening concerts were so popular that special trains ran from Antwerp and Brussels.

Other cities, like Bruges, copied the idea. Its concerts attracted many tourists, including the American writer Henry Longfellow, who dedicated two poems to the carillon – *The Belfry of Bruges* and *Carillon*.

Denyn went on to set up the world's first carillon school in Mechelen in 1922. It received funding from several wealthy American donors including Herbert Hoover and John D. Rockefeller Jr. The school now occupies a former Norbertine priory in the heart of Mechelen.

You can often tell a carilloneur from their bandaged hands. The injuries are caused by the karate-like technique they use to strike the keys. It's a tough life up in those windy towers. But these musicians provide a reassuring soundtrack for daily life in Belgium. It wouldn't be the same without them.

Monuments au
Pigeon-Soldat

—

Quai aux Barques 1
Brussels

—

Parc Reine Astrid
Charleroi

PIGEON RACING

The curious sport of pigeon racing was invented in Belgium in 1818, three years after the Battle of Waterloo. It involved training pigeons to fly home to their loft from a starting point over 100 kilometres away.

The new sport spread to France and Great Britain, with a race organised from Paris to Belgium in 1820, and from London to Belgium three years later. It caught on in other countries, but nowhere in the world has embraced the sport more than Belgium, where almost every village had its pigeon lofts and local pigeon-fanciers' club.

Pigeons have been known to cover distances of several thousand kilometres, sometimes at speeds of almost 150 km/h. The trained homing pigeons turned out to be a vital military asset during the First World War when they were used to deliver urgent messages and take aerial photographs. Some were even regarded as war heroes because of their bravery.

In 1931, a bronze statue was unveiled in the centre of Brussels in memory of the pigeons and pigeon-fanciers who lost their lives in the war. It shows a young woman symbolising Belgium as she releases a pigeon into the sky.

It is one of only three monuments in the world dedicated to the pigeon soldiers of the First World War. The other two are in Charleroi and Lille in northern France.

VOIL JEANETTEN

Once a year, grey industrial Aalst goes insane. No one can explain, but this modest industrial town north of Brussels has one of the most outrageous carnivals in the world. It includes a parade of floats that merciless mock the political events of the past year and a ceremony during which onions are hurled down from the belfry.

But that's not the strangest part. On Mardi Gras, thousands of local men parade through the streets dressed as women. They don't just wear a dress and some lipstick. The dedicated *Voil Jeanetten* (Dirty Jeanies) put together bizarre costumes involving false breasts and fur coats, along with antiquated prams, dead herrings in bird cages and vintage lampshades.

The Voil Jeanetten parade goes back to the 19th century when local men were often too poor to afford a carnival costume. So they would improvise by raiding their wives' wardrobes and adding something absurd like a broken umbrella.

The Jeanetten normally have a drink or two before setting off so the parade can get rowdy. Some carry chamber pots filled with a mix of *speculoos* and beer. Others will try to whack you in the face with a dead fish.

It is meant to be fun, but it isn't always funny. Sometimes the joke falls flat. Sometimes people are upset. But Aalst refuses to change. And everyone returns to work the next morning in this industrial town as if carnival never happened.

Saint Sebastian's Guild
Carmersstraat 174
Bruges
+32 (0)50 33 16 26
sebastiaansgilde.be

VERTICAL ARCHERY

It sounds like a joke, but vertical archery is a serious sport in Belgium that goes back several centuries. Known as *wipschieten* in Dutch, or popinjay in English, it involves shooting a wooden 'bird' off the top of a 28-metre-high iron mast. Obviously, it takes some skill to avoid getting hit by the bird, or the arrow, or both.

The country is dotted with special masts built for *wipschieten*. Some training grounds include a wooden archery tower to allow the sport to carry on in winter. You find an archery tower in Rixensart with a small museum attached. But the world's oldest vertical archery society is in Bruges. Founded more than 600 years ago, the Guild of Saint Sebastian still practises vertical archery in a garden behind its beautiful meeting hall.

OMMEGANG

On any given day, there is probably a procession happening somewhere in Belgium. It might be the giants' parade in Ath, or the cats parade in Ypres, or men walking through Ghent with nooses around their necks. Anything is possible.

Some processions are religious, dating back to the Middle Ages, like the Holy Blood Procession in Bruges. Others are held to commemorate historical events, such as the Meiboom Procession in Brussels, when local men carry an enormous tree trunk through the cobbled streets.

The annual Brussels Ommegang is one of the most spectacular processions in Europe. Held on two nights in July, the parade features more than 1400 people dressed in rich historical costumes. There are archers, crossbowmen, flag-wavers, stilt walkers, giants, dancers, children and horses. It ends on Grand-Place just after the sun goes down with a fireworks display that lights up the night sky.

People describe it as a mediaeval procession, but like many things in Belgium it's more complicated than it looks. The current version of the Ommegang was first enacted in 1930 to mark the 100th anniversary of the Belgian revolution. The concept was carefully choreographed by a local historian after he sifted through the city archives looking for an ancient procession that might be revived.

He eventually came across an exceptionally lavish version of the mediaeval Ommegang procession held in the summer of 1549 to celebrate the visit of Charles V and his son Philip. This was exactly what the city needed to draw the crowds.

The modern Ommegang follows roughly the same route as the 1549 procession, from the church of Notre-Dame du Sablon down through the narrow cobbled lanes to Grand-Place. The participants include aristocratic descendants of the nobles who took part in the original 1549 procession. You can book a seat on Grand-Place to watch the final ceremony, or just join the crowds lining the route.

NATIONAL ANTHEM

When the Belgian football team sing the national anthem at the start of a game, the players often seem confused about the words. And you can't really blame them, because there are four different versions.

It was a lot simpler when the country was created in 1830. The exiled French actor Jenneval scribbled down some inspiring words in an upstairs room of the cafe L'Aigle d'Or while the revolution was being fought in the streets down below. The score was written by François Van Campenhout based on an old drinking song. It was called *La Brabançonne,* and sung in French, the national language at the time.

The text was later revised by various committees, cut down to one verse, and translated into Dutch and German. "*Ô Belgique, ô mère chérie*" – O Belgium, o mother dear, they sing in Wallonia. "*O liebes Land, o Belgiens Erde*" – O dear country, o Belgium's soil, they learn in school in the German region of Belgium. "*O dierbaar België, o heilig land der vaad'ren*" – O dear Belgium, o holy land of the fathers, is sung in Flanders.

The opening verse is carved on the pedestal of the *La Brabançonne* statue in Brussels. Originally it was only in French. Now there is also a Dutch version. And that's not the end of it. There is also a trilingual version of the national anthem that has become popular on Belgian National Day. Twelve lines long, the anthem switches from Dutch to French to German.

So it's complicated. With four national and two regional anthems, it's difficult to know what to sing. When Yves Leterme, a candidate prime minister, was asked in a television interview on Belgium's National Day in 2007 if he knew the national anthem, he smiled, and started to sing the French national anthem.

Yet Leterme still became prime minister. "Maybe it's positive that nationalism doesn't exist in Belgium," wrote the journalist Bernard Bulcke. "So we can't sing the national anthem. Who cares?"

THE LAST POST

There is nothing like this anywhere in the world. Every evening at just before 8 pm, the traffic is halted on Menenstraat in Ypres. Two local firemen then raise their bugles to play the *Last Post* below the Menin Gate war memorial.

This sad military call was first performed in Ypres by British buglers at the unveiling of the Menin Gate on 24 July 1927. The local police chief was so moved that he set up a committee to ensure the *Last Post* was played every evening by local volunteer firemen.

The buglers have performed every day since 2 June 1928, more than 32.000 times, apart from the period under German Occupation from 1940 to 1944. Just hours after Polish troops liberated Ypres on 6 September 1944, Jozef Arfeuille grabbed his bugle and rushed to the Menin Gate with a group of friends. According to witnesses, he repeated the call six times that evening.

The *Last Post* was originally intended to commemorate over 54.000 missing soldiers from Britain and the Commonwealth listed on the Menin Gate. But it has grown over the years into a ceremony to commemorate all the dead of the First World War.

Sometimes the buglers play to a few tourists. Other days, huge crowds gather under the gate. "It is the intention of the Last Post Association to maintain this daily act of homage in perpetuity," the website declares.

ICONIC
places

De Kat
Wolstraat 22
Antwerp
+32 (0)3 233 08 92

In de Verzekering
tegen de Grote Dorst
Frans Baetensstraat 45
Eizeringen (Lennik)
+32 (0)2 532 58 58
dorst.be

OLD BELGIAN CAFES

The Belgian cafe is a special place. You push open the stiff front door to find it is filled with regulars drinking strong Belgian beers and talking in a local dialect you don't understand. The walls are stained a dark brown colour as a reminder of the days when smoking was tolerated.

These places sometimes seem a little intimidating. But that's just the way they look. You find a seat and ask for a drink. Maybe a coffee if there is coffee. Or a beer, something strong, a Duvel or an Orval, even in the morning, if you want to blend in with the locals.

Many of these traditional cafes are located in the front room of a house. The interior is decorated with wood-panelling, a tiled floor, some mirrors along the wall, a row of tough green plants on the window ledge that block out the grey Belgian daylight.

These old cafes often serve as meeting places for local associations. Possibly a cycle club, or a group of pigeon fanciers, or a football supporters' association. Locals go there to play cards on rainy afternoons, or perhaps a game of skittles in the backyard, or to drown their sorrows after a funeral.

De Kat in Antwerp is a typical old cafe. It stands on a street corner where tram number 11 rumbles past the window. The interior is quite plain with a tiled floor, wood-panelled walls and an ancient piano that hasn't been tuned in a while.

The cafe In de Verzekering tegen de Grote Dorst has stood on the village square of Eizeringen since the 1840s. It is just a plain local cafe with an art deco bar and an old English clock, but in 2014 it was voted best beer bar in the world by the beer website *ratebeer.com*. Ever since then, it has been thronged with beer fans from all over the world who have learned to pronounce the long name and memorise the short opening hours (Sundays from 10 am to 8 pm).

Gruuthusemuseum
Dijver 12
Bruges
+32 (0)50 44 87 43
museabrugge.be

BRUGES

Bruges is a strange town. Most guidebooks describe it as a perfectly preserved mediaeval town, but it isn't. Not at all. The Belgian historian Roel Jacobs once counted up the number of authentic mediaeval houses in Bruges. He only found two wooden houses built in the Middle Ages.

Bruges is not as old as it looks, Jacobs argued in his 1997 book *Brugge, een stad in de geschiedenis*. Many of the buildings that appear Gothic were built by English architects in the 19th century. The most famous bridge in the city looks as if it has been there for hundreds of years, but it was actually constructed in 1909 partly using old gravestones. While the rest of Belgium was building factories and railway stations, architects in Bruges were busy constructing a mediaeval fantasy.

Tourists started flooding the streets in the late 19th century. Many wanted to visit the city after reading Georges Rodenbach's haunting 1892 novella *Bruges-la-Morte*. Illustrated with photographs of the dead city, it told the story of a grieving man who moved to Bruges after his wife died.

The city has never liked the novel because of its morbid theme (and because it was written in French). It's hard to find a copy of the book in local bookshops, or any monument to Rodenbach, apart from a small plaque on a house where he never lived. The city prefers to market itself as 'Brugge-die-Schone', Bruges-the-Beautiful.

When the comedy gangster film *In Bruges* was released in 2008, everyone assumed the tourist office would be upset. But they loved it. They gave it a special place on their website and published a guide to the film locations, even though one of the characters said he would rather be dead than in Bruges.

THE BELGIAN COAST

Most people say the same thing. The Belgian coast is ugly. It is just a long line of apartment buildings overlooking a grey sea. They call it the Atlantic Wall (although it is on the North Sea). It rains almost every day, they will tell you. The waiters are rude. The wind blows sand in your face. And so it goes on. No one has a good word to say about the Belgian coast and yet millions visit it every year. Mostly Belgians from Brussels and Wallonia, but also Germans and even a few French. Many Belgians have a family apartment in one of the 13 resorts with a sea view if they are lucky.

The little towns are lively places with restaurants serving mussels, cafes where you can order waffles, souvenir shops that sell beach umbrellas. A few of the beach towns have kept their old romantic charm, like De Haan and Het Zoute. You might even spot an art nouveau villa in Blankenberge or Ostend.

No one pretends the Belgian beach is elegant, except maybe the mayor of Knokke, who has tried to ban picnic boxes, bikinis in the streets and music on the beach. Other resorts are more relaxed. Sometimes ugly. But often charming.

Doel
Antwerp
doel2020.org

ABANDONED PLACES

Every country has abandoned places, but Belgium has more than most. You come across countless ruined factories in the old industrial regions around Liege, Charleroi and Aalst. You also find churches, castles and department stores that no one cares for any longer.

Many of the country's abandoned buildings date from the 19th century when Belgium was an economic superpower. The wealth was used to build houses and public buildings on an epic scale. These buildings are now impossible to maintain. No one wants to buy an enormous castle with a leaky roof or a huge town house with an overgrown garden in the centre of Charleroi.

You sometimes find an entire abandoned village, like Doel, near Antwerp, which was evacuated in the 1960s to build a dock that never happened. Over the years, its empty houses have been sprayed with graffiti to create a strange dystopian setting. Less well known, the village of Sur-les-Bois lies abandoned at the end of an airport runway in Liège province.

Sometimes an abandoned place will be saved. But often the buildings are left to rot until they are finally torn down.

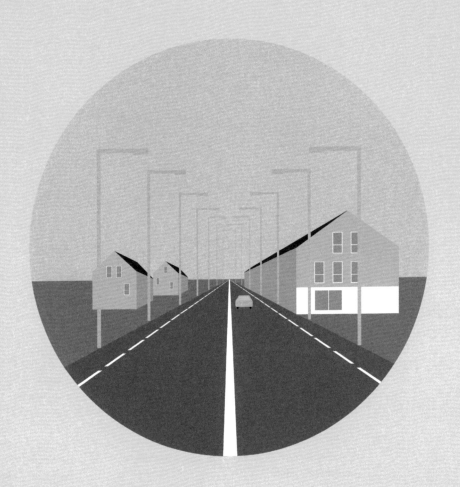

N ROADS

The N roads are the lost highways of Belgium. Built in the 1950s to link the main cities, they were once a symbol of the future. These long straight roads lined with sleek lamps marked the beginning of the age of car travel, when Belgians would set off on their summer vacation to the coast or the Ardennes.

The inspiration came from America. Belgians have been obsessed by the American dream since the 1920s, but the country really began to fall for the American suburban lifestyle in the 1960s. A country of city dwellers became a country of commuters.

It seems odd now, but people moved into new houses conveniently located on the N roads. These suburban villas were built in weird, eclectic styles with front windows that now look out on an endless stream of traffic.

These houses on N roads have become impossible to sell. They end up being converted into garages, or night shops or roadside brothels. But a few are still inhabited by people who came in search of the American dream.

Baraque Michel
Baraque Michel 36
Jalhay
+32 (0)80 44 48 01
baraquemichel.com

La Maison du
Parc-Botrange
Route de Botrange 131
Waimes
+32 (0)80 44 03 00
botrange.be

HAUTES FAGNES

Anyone who says Belgium is flat and boring has never been to the Hautes Fagnes. This is one of the wildest upland regions in northern Europe, marked by misty hills, dark forests and boggy marshes. "Snow half the year, bad weather half the year," observed a professor from Brussels who decided to renovate the ruined Reinhardstein castle on the edge of the moors.

Rainfall here is twice the national average. Even in summer, the mist can come down suddenly, wrapping everything in a sinister silence. The long-distance hiking trail GR 573 crosses this bleak upland region where nothing much can survive apart from tough heather and isolated pine trees. The GR trail passes the Signal de Botrange. This is the highest spot in Belgium, 694 metres above sea level.

The Hautes Fagnes is a culturally confusing region with a mix of Belgian and German influences. It used to be Prussian up until the end of the First World War. Then it became Belgian. It's hardly surprising it feels such a strange, lost place.

No one lives in this cold, marshy region of Europe. You sometimes have to walk along raised wooden walkways to avoid the waterlogged marshes, and at one point pass a cross where two lovers died in a storm. As you tramp across the moorland, you can see a rich variety of rare species growing in this unique habitat. You might also, if you are lucky, spot deer, a fox or maybe even a family of wild boar.

One of the few buildings in this desolate region is the ancient inn called Baraque Michel where travellers have been sheltering from the wind and rain for centuries. It's a rustic German-style place with heavy wood tables, an old stove and baskets filled with logs. The perfect spot for some Ardennes home cooking and a glass of the house beer.

Hoffy's Restaurant	Kleinblatt
Lange Kievitstraat 52	Provinciestraat 206
Antwerp	Antwerp
+32 (0)3 234 35 35	+32 (0)3 233 75 13
hoffys.be	*kleinblatt.be*

ANTWERP JEWISH QUARTER

It looks drab and underwhelming, but Antwerp's Jewish quarter is an intriguing urban district. Located close to the magnificent Central Station, the neighbourhood is crammed into a warren of dark, narrow streets such as Pelikaanstraat and Hoveniersstraat. This is where you find most of the world's diamond dealers, along with kosher restaurants, wig shops and family bakeries.

The Jewish community in Antwerp goes back to the Middle Ages when Jews were driven out of England, France, Spain and Portugal. They often found work in the diamond industry when other professions refused to admit them. The population rapidly expanded in the 19th century as exiles arrived from Eastern Europe, while a further wave reached Antwerp from Germany in the 1930s.

During the Nazi occupation, thousands of Jews were deported from Antwerp. But the Jewish quarter didn't disappear. After the war, the Jews who survived returned here to rebuild their lives. About 20.000 Jews now live in Antwerp. Some are strictly Orthodox while others are more relaxed. There are about 30 synagogues dotted around, along with Jewish schools, newspapers and shops.

While Jews no longer dominate the Antwerp diamond industry, they still live in the Pelikaan neighbourhood. It's a fascinating district to wander around, with its shops selling traditional black hats, kosher delicatessens and diamond cutting-tool suppliers.

BATTLEFIELDS

This small country has suffered endlessly because of its location between Europe's great powers. Its towns have often lent their names to famous battles. Sometimes more than one. There are three battles in the First World War named after Ypres, and no fewer than seven battles of Kortrijk, from the first in 1302 to the most recent at the end of the First World War.

Occasionally, you find an information panel, a monument, or a small museum. But often there is nothing left of the battlefield apart from a name that has entered Europe's history books – Ramillies or Oudenaarde or Passchendaele.

Belgium's almost endless history of violence is reflected in the enormous military collection held by the Military History Museum in Brussels. Located in a former 19th-century exhibition hall, the museum displays weapons, uniforms, flags, maps, tanks and aircraft. It has a huge collection of objects from the First World War, along with a new section that opened in 2019 dedicated to the occupation and liberation of Belgium, and an unexpected Russian Gallery filled with weapons and other objects carried by officers who fled the Russian Revolution.

Galerie de la Porte
de Namur
Chaussée d'Ixelles 1
Ixelles

MATONGE

It is strange to come upon an African quarter in the heart of Brussels' fashionable Ixelles district. Originally a 19th-century neighbourhood, the quarter has gradually acquired an African identity due to its close links with Belgium's former colonies.

It began in the late 1950s when a Belgian woman opened a hostel in Ixelles for Congolese visitors to Expo 58. Then students began to arrive in the neighbourhood. They called it Matonge after a district in Kinshasa. The exclusive shopping arcade Galerie d'Ixelles slowly changed as stores were taken over by African barber shops, Congolese record stores and beauty parlours.

There is nowhere like it in Europe. The streets are full of people from a dozen different African countries who have settled in Brussels, along with tourists who come to pick up African specialities or do business.

An important ceremony took place in 2018 when a small square in the Matonge was named Square Patrice Lumumba. It honours the first leader of the Congo, who was murdered in 1961.

It is a miracle the Matonge has survived. It sits in a desirable neighbourhood, bordered by the Royal Palace, the European quarter and the stylish Avenue Louise. Many Africans have moved away. But it still has an African spirit, especially on a hot night in the summer.

House of
European History
Rue Belliard 135
Brussels
+32 (0)2 283 12 20
historia-europa.ep.eu

BRUSSELS BUBBLE

The most important European Union institutions are concentrated in a small Brussels neighbourhood near the Cinquantenaire Park. The 'Brussels bubble', as it is called, is dominated by office buildings, busy roads and police barriers. A bit like Washington DC. People come here from all over the world to attend meetings, but hardly anyone goes there as a tourist. Why would you want to do that? Yet this is a fascinating neighbourhood, rich in history and architecture, dotted with parks, museums, restaurants and cafes.

More than 80.000 jobs in Brussels are linked to the European Union, according to the most recent figures (from 2016). They include 40.000 people employed by the EU, 5500 based at NATO and Eurocontrol, 5400 diplomats, 20.000 lobbyists and more than 1000 journalists.

The main sights in this city within a city include the 1960s Berlaymont building, where the European Commission is based, the Europa building and the European Parliament. The people who work in these buildings have everything they need. Many do not ever leave the bubble.

The House of European History is the place to go to understand the history of Europe. Opened in 2017 in a former dental hospital on the edge of Parc Leopold, it sets out to tell the story of Europe using objects and documents from 300 European collections. The presentation is ambitious and innovative, using digital tablets with texts in all 24 EU languages. The extensive collection covers two world wars, the Cold War period and even the 2016 Brexit referendum.

CHARLEROI

When Dutch newspaper *De Volkskrant* asked its readers in 2008 to name the ugliest place in the world, they chose the Belgian city of Charleroi, followed by Liège in second place.

Most Belgians would agree that Charleroi is a dreadful place, even if they have never been there. It is an old industrial town in the heart of *Le Pays Noir,* the Black Country, surrounded by abandoned steelworks, coal tips and grim streets.

The Charleroi-born artist Nicolas Buissart responded to the criticism by launching 'city safari tours' in a van with no seats. He took little groups of adventurous tourists to the most horrendous spots in the city, including ghost metro stations, the river where Magritte's mother committed suicide, the top of a slag heap, and 'the most depressing street in Belgium'.

But a lot has changed since the *Volkskrant* poll. The city has created a waterfront promenade, a gleaming shopping centre and a stunning museum of photography. Buissart has gone on to suggest Charleroi is 'the new Berlin' where artists and musicians are bringing fresh energy to the industrial ruins.

It will never be the most beautiful place in Europe, but Charleroi could be one of the most interesting cities of the 21st century.

Le Circuit de
Spa-Francorchamps
Route du Circuit 55
Francorchamps
+32 (0)87 29 37 00
spa-francorchamps.be

Musée du Circuit
AT: Abbaye de Stavelot
Cour de l'Abbaye
Stavelot
+32 (0)80 86 42 61
musee-circuit.be

SPA-FRANCORCHAMPS

It has been described as the most beautiful car racing circuit in the world, but also the most dangerous. Every year, the Spa-Francorchamps circuit brings the roar of Formula One to the remote Ardennes hills. The three-day race attracts at least 250.000 fans, who occupy every last hotel room in the region, while 200 million watch on TV.

Established soon after the First World War, the original circuit was designed by local newspaper proprietor Jules de Thier and racing driver Henri Langlois van Ophem. They mapped out the 15,8-kilometre route on a triangle of rough local roads connecting the towns of Stavelot, Malmédy and Francorchamps. The name Spa was added to bring a touch of glamour to the race.

The first competition was scheduled for 1921, but only one driver signed up, and a motorbike race was held instead. The following year, the first car race took place. The route ran through dark pine woods, past white farmhouses and an old German border post.

The Spa-Francorchamps circuit has always been a dangerous, romantic challenge. Some drivers love it. Others curse the circuit. The unreliable Ardennes weather can suddenly change from sunshine to heavy rain. The notorious bends with names like Raidillon à l'Eau Rouge, Les Combes and Blanchimont are known to millions of fans across the world.

In its 100 years, more than 50 drivers have died on the circuit. Following a spate of deadly accidents, crash barriers were installed for the first time in 1963, and in 1979 the race was moved to a new 6,9-kilometre circuit.

The F1 cars no longer scream along the local roads around Francorchamps. But you can still drive on sections of the old circuit where the world's best drivers once hit speeds of over 300 kilometres an hour.

ICONIC
history

**Museum of
Natural Sciences**
Rue Vautier 29
Brussels
+32 (0)2 627 42 27
naturalsciences.be

THE BERNISSART DINOSAURS

It isn't easy to find the Museum of Natural Sciences in Brussels. You need to follow the small signs illustrated with a cartoon dinosaur. They lead to an impressive science museum where Europe's largest dinosaur collection is displayed.

It all began in 1878 in the Walloon mining village of Bernissart, not far from the French border, when a coal miner working deep underground hit something unexpected. He thought it was gold, but it turned out to be a dinosaur bone.

Eventually archaeologists uncovered about 30 intact skeletons of iguanodons buried at a depth of 322 metres. Using a complicated system of ropes and pulleys, the celebrated palaeontologist Louis Dollo carefully assembled the skeletons in the 15th-century Nassau chapel in Brussels.

Untouched for 125 million years, the fossils gave 19th-century scientists their first accurate impression of dinosaurs. The skeletons are now displayed in a beautiful 19th-century glass gallery surrounded by viewing platforms reached by ornate spiral staircases.

Scientists have proposed several theories to explain how the 30 dinosaurs died. They might have drowned in marshes, or fallen off a cliff, or simply died of natural causes. In 2015 the museum launched a new project called Cold Case involving scientists from Brussels and Mons universities. Their aim is to solve this 125-million-year-old mystery.

Mémorial Waterloo 1815
Route du Lion 1815
Braine-l'Alleud
+32 (0)2 385 19 12
waterloo1815.be

WATERLOO

Most Belgians don't care about Waterloo. And why should they? It was a victory for an Allied army composed of troops from Britain, Germany and the Netherlands. Belgium wasn't even a country at the time.

It matters more to the British, who went on to name hundreds of places 'Waterloo' in honour of the victory, including a railway station in London, a square in Edinburgh, and more than 100 towns across the British Empire, from Australia to Canada.

The Germans also remember the battle, which they call 'La Belle Alliance', after a local inn where General Blücher ended the day. A square in Berlin is called Belle-Alliance-Platz because of the battle. Meanwhile, the French, who lost, naturally say nothing.

The Belgians are somewhere in the middle. Some fought for the French, the revolutionaries. Others were on the side of the Allies, protecting the old order. Most just kept their heads down, so it is difficult to know what to do with the battlefield.

It didn't matter too much in the beginning, as the Dutch ruled over this region of Europe. They knew precisely what had to be done, which was to construct a large earth pyramid on the spot where the young Prince of Orange was wounded.

But then the Belgians took over the site and it became a mess. They built a couple of restaurants, a hotel and a panorama building. There were also car parks, a go kart circuit and of course a *friterie*.

Eventually, Waterloo battlefield was acquired by a French company that specialises in historical sites. The car park was removed. The old restaurants closed down. The ugly *friterie* demolished. It is now a spectacular historical site with military demonstrations in the summer.

Train World
Place Princesse Elisabeth 5
Schaerbeek
+32 (0)2 224 74 37
trainworld.be

Paul Delvaux Museum
Paul Delvauxlaan 42
+32 (0)58 52 12 29
Sint-Idesbald
delvauxmuseum.be

BELGIAN RAILWAYS

Belgium has a long history of train travel. It was the second country in the world to build a railway. In 1835, just five years after independence, the country had laid down tracks between Brussels and Mechelen. The first steam train to run on mainland Europe was proudly named 'Le Belge', the Belgian.

Two years later, the French writer Victor Hugo described a night journey on the route that by then had reached Antwerp. "It was the most terrifying thing," he wrote to his wife, after he had seen a train pass in the opposite direction. "You could see neither carriages nor passengers, just black and white shapes in a sort of whirlwind."

The young nation wanted to put itself at the heart of a European rail network, despite some anxiety about trains causing milk to curdle and eggs to turn into omelettes. An enthusiastic government went on to construct Europe's densest railway network with lines running out to the coast and deep into the Ardennes. Soon the tracks extended beyond the Belgian borders to Paris, Berlin and Vienna.

Fascinated by Belgian train stations, the surrealist artist Paul Delvaux captured their strange mood in many of his works. He painted antiquated railway stations at night with statuesque naked women and small girls in 19th-century dresses. Some of his works are hung in the Paul Delvaux Museum in the beach village of Sint-Idesbald, in a modern building next to the cottage where he lived for many years.

The history of Belgian railways is presented in a stunning new museum called Train World located in an abandoned station next to the railway tracks in the Brussels suburb of Schaerbeek. Designed by the comic book artist Francois Schuiten, the museum incorporates a fascinating collection of locomotives, carriages and equipment in a series of giant sheds. The dark spotlit spaces are filled with a mix of train sounds and music that add further depth to the experience.

CONGO

Belgium has been linked to the Congo since 1885 when Leopold II secured a vast colony in central Africa, eighty times the size of Belgium, named the Congo Free State. Originally exploited as King Leopold's private territory, and taken over by the Belgian state in 1908, the Congo brought enormous wealth to Belgium, including ivory, rubber, coffee and cocoa. But Leopold's rule was catastrophic for the local population, leading to the deaths of millions of Africans.

Belgium is dotted with Leopold's grand architectural projects, built with money from the Congo, including the Palais de Justice and the royal greenhouses in Brussels, Central Station in Antwerp and the Royal Galleries in Ostend.

Leopold also constructed the Africa Museum in Tervuren to showcase the riches of his colony. He commissioned a French architect to design a grand palace in the style of Versailles. It was intended to give Belgians a thrilling glimpse of the distant colony's mineral resources, wild animals and natural wonders.

But the country has recently started to take a more critical view of Leopold's colony. This can be seen in the redesign of the Africa Museum which reopened in 2019 after a sweeping five-year renovation. The museum is now entered through a striking glass pavilion designed by Stéphane Beel with windows looking out on the Tervuren woods.

The vast collection built up during the colonial years has been radically reorganised to focus on African culture, nature and history. Leopold's influence is finally fading in Belgium, as African voices begin to tell the true story.

Tyne Cot Cemetery
Vijfwegestraat
Zonnebeke
toerismezonnebeke.be

**Vladslo German
Cemetery**
Houtlandstraat 3
Diksmuide

WAR CEMETERIES

Most people who visit the Belgian cemeteries of the First World War head to Tyne Cot, where the sheer scale of the killing is reflected in the endless rows of white gravestones. Yet there are 140 cemeteries around the town of Ypres. The smaller cemeteries – some with just a few dozen graves – are hardly visited at all. But they have a special atmosphere because of their location in the landscape where the soldiers fought and died.

At the end of the First World War, tens of thousands of bodies lay scattered across the landscape. Some were buried in graves dug along the line of battle. Others simply disappeared into the muddy soil.

The Imperial War Graves Commission was set up in 1917 to come up with a more dignified method for burying so many dead. The architect Edwin Lutyens drew up a plan that led to the creation of the war cemeteries.

The small cemeteries are often in isolated spots that are hard to reach. You might need to rent a bike in Ypres. Or hike down a muddy track. But these little cemeteries offer a unique insight into the war.

There are also a few scattered German war cemeteries. Not many. The local farmers weren't too keen to surrender their farmland to the enemy. The dead are crammed into graves that contain six or eight bodies. They are gloomy places where almost no one comes. Yet they tell the same story of futility and suffering.

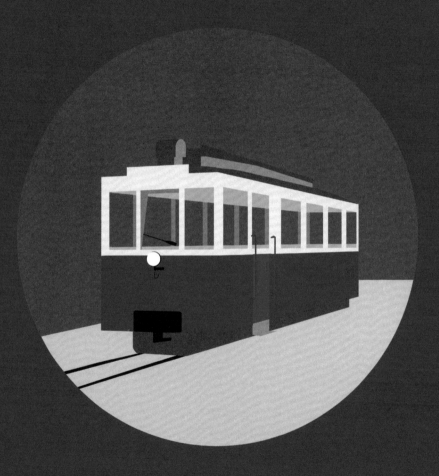

Tram Museum
Avenue de Tervuren 364-B
Woluwe-Saint-Pierre
+32 (0)2 515 31 08
trammuseum.brussels

Grottes de Han
Rue Joseph Lamotte 2
Han-sur-Lesse
+32 (0)84 37 72 13
grotte-de-han.be

TRAMS

Most countries tore up their tram lines in the 1960s, but Belgium was slow to follow the trend. It means you can take a tram for 68 kilometres along the Belgian coast, or through the forest outside Brussels, or deep into the mediaeval heart of Ghent.

It's hard to explain, but there's something romantic about a tram ride. The tinny clang of the bell as it sets off, the seats so close together that no one knows where to put their knees, the well-dressed ladies clutching a small poodle, the endless fascinating views as the tram winds through the city streets of Brussels or Ghent.

Belgium also constructed rural tramlines in the 1880s to link small towns and villages without a railway line. By the 1920s, rural trams rumbled along more than 4000 kilometres of track, stopping along the way outside the village church and the local cafe.

In the late 1950s, the government decided that cars were the future, and the entire rural tram network was dug up. Some old tramlines were turned into cycle trails, but others have vanished completely.

The only survivor is the ancient tram that runs from the village of Han-sur-Lesse in the Ardennes. The tracks were laid in 1906 to take visitors to the caves above the village. It's now a nostalgic ride for tourists in ancient red and cream coaches with hard wooden benches.

Bastogne War Museum
Colline du Mardasson 5
Bastogne
+32 (0)61 21 02 20
bastognewarmuseum.be

Le Nut's
Place Général Mac Auliffe 3
Bastogne
+32 (0)61 68 96 88
lenutsbastogne.com

BASTOGNE

"Nuts!"

One word spoken in Bastogne in the winter of 1944 sums up the last great battle fought in Western Europe. General Anthony McAuliffe of the United States army was responding to a German ultimatum to surrender the besieged Belgian town of Bastogne. His laconic reply was eagerly reported by the American press. And the modest town of Bastogne became famous as the site of the single most important battle in American history, dramatised in several Hollywood war movies as well as in the TV series *Band of Brothers*.

Deep in the Ardennes, Bastogne lay at the heart of the Battle of the Bulge. Fought in freezing temperatures from 16 December 1944 to 25 January 1945, the epic battle raged across a small area of Belgium known as 'The Bulge' where the German army tried to break through American lines. It ended with the German army finally defeated in Belgium at a cost of 19.000 American soldiers and 2500 Belgian civilians.

A huge American monument on a hill above Bastogne commemorates the soldiers who fought in the battle. The dark forests around the town are dotted with war cemeteries, monuments and abandoned tanks. You often come across old photographs from the war in local cafes and hotels.

But there are other less visible traces of war around the bulge. A series of 26 marker stones were placed along the edge of the bulge in the 1950s to mark the line where the German attack was halted. On one side of the road, you see old Ardennes farmhouses dating back several hundred years. On the opposite side, where the fighting happened, all the buildings are modern.

You also come across some strange souvenirs of the battle, such as a restaurant called Le Nut's, on Place Général Mac Auliffe in Bastogne, opposite an American tank.

136

Salon 58
Avenue de l'Atomium 6
Laeken
+32 (0)2 479 84 00
salon58.com

EXPO 58

Nearly every home in Belgium has something from Expo 58. It might be a shiny ashtray, or a photo album, or a souvenir pen. Some families even have old home movies from that summer of 1958 stored away in the attic.

The Brussels World Fair happened more than 60 years ago, but older Belgians still have fond memories of Expo 58. Held on the Heysel heights to the north of the city, it was the first major international event in Europe after the Second World War. The national pavilions reflected a desire for international cooperation, scientific progress and growing prosperity. The Americans and the Russians presented their competing world views in spectacular buildings. The new international bodies such as the Benelux, the United Nations and the newly created European Steel and Coal Community (which would eventually become the European Union) set up pavilions to spread their message.

But Expo 58 was mostly about fun. Visitors could take a ride above the site in little blue cable car cabins, eat Belgian waffles, drink Belgian beers. More than 42 million visitors flocked to the exhibition site. Four out of five Belgians visited the fair, and some went several times. It was a turning point for this small country. People discovered an exciting new world, new architecture, a new way of living. And it put Brussels on the map as a city dedicated to science, progress and good living.

Most of the buildings were torn down as soon as the fair ended in the autumn of 1958. The only relics to survive at the site were the Atomium, the circular American pavilion and a quirky building put up by the Kortrijk textile association – now restaurant Salon 58. But the real legacy of Expo 58 was to turn Belgium into a modern country with fast highways, sleek architecture and sweet waffles.

ICONIC
art & artists

Rubenshuis
Wapper 9-11
Antwerp
+32 (0)3 201 15 55
rubenshuis.be

RUBENS

Everything about Rubens is oversized, from his Italian-style villa in the heart of Antwerp to the baroque triumphal arch he built in the back garden. His monumental importance is obvious the moment you step inside the Rubenshuis museum in Antwerp. Even the studio where he turned out more than 1400 paintings is enormous.

As well as all the paintings, Rubens worked as an architect, a diplomat and a spy. He brought the Italian baroque style to Flanders and helped to negotiate a peace treaty between England and Spain. His paintings have inspired countless other European artists, from Delacroix to Constable and even Van Gogh.

That's maybe the problem with Rubens. He was just too big, too successful, too flamboyant. When people talk about *Rubenesque*, they don't mean it as a compliment. It suggests a plump, fleshy woman, like the portrait of his young second wife Hélène Fourment posing in nothing more than a fur cloak. Some of Rubens' paintings have so much bare flesh that they have been censored by Facebook.

Rubens produced hundreds of exceptional works, from the *Descent from the Cross* in Antwerp Cathedral to intimate sketches of his children that are seldom shown in museums. He was undoubtedly the greatest Belgian artist. But maybe he was a little too great for this modest country.

art & artists   **Old Masters Museum**   **Bruegel mural**
                  Rue de la Régence 3   Rue du Chevreuil 14-16
                  Brussels   Brussels
                  +32 (0)2 508 32 11
                  fine-arts-museum.be

BRUEGEL

Pieter Bruegel the Elder was an astonishingly versatile artist whose works ranged from crowded paintings representing old Netherlandish proverbs to weird drawings of imaginary fish and birds.

He was born somewhere in the Low Countries. No one knows the place. Or the year. He began working as an artist in Antwerp and then moved to Brussels in 1563, married his teacher's daughter, and died in 1569.

Along the way, he changed the spelling of his name from Brueghel to Bruegel. And, to add to the confusion, he had two sons who were artists, Pieter and Jan, who restored the old spelling of Brueghel.

Pieter Bruegel the Elder's name is attached to about 45 paintings and 65 drawings. But only a few works remain in Belgium. His painting *Landscape with the Fall of Icarus* is in the Fine Arts Museum in Brussels, while his *Dulle Griet* is in the Mayer van den Bergh Museum in Antwerp. Most of his famous works – like the *Wedding Feast* and *The Tower of Babel* – are in foreign collections.

There was once a plan to create a Bruegel museum in a 16th-century Brussels house. A plaque on the outside wall records that Bruegel lived in the house at Rue Haute 123 from 1563 until his death in 1569. Only it turns out he didn't live in the house. And so the plan was dropped.

Pieter Bruegel was buried in (or possibly near) the church of Notre Dame de la Chapelle in the Marolles district of Brussels. To mark the 450th anniversary of his death, several street artists were commissioned to paint murals inspired by Bruegel's works. A strange bronze statue was placed outside Notre Dame de la Chapelle by the Brussels sculptor Tom Frantzen. It shows the bearded artist sitting at his easel. A monkey wearing a funnel as a hat is perched on his shoulder. Bruegel would probably have enjoyed the joke.

| *art & artists*   **René Magritte Museum**   **Magritte Museum**
Rue Esseghem 135   Place Royale
Jette   Brussels
+32 (0)2 428 26 26   +32 (0)2 508 32 11
magrittemuseum.be   *musee-magritte-*
museum.be

MAGRITTE

'Magritte,' it says on the doorbell of a terraced house in a quiet Brussels suburb. You ring the bell tentatively, wondering if it will be answered by a man in a bowler hat. The door opens and you enter the former home of Belgium's most famous 20th-century artist.

Magritte may have been one of the great artists of the 20th century, but he looked like a dull civil servant. He lived a boring life of bourgeois respectability in a house furnished with replica Louis XVI furniture, along with his wife Georgette and a fluffy white Pomeranian dog. He even wore a suit and tie when he was working on a painting. How surreal, you might think.

Even more surreal is the fact that Brussels has two Magritte museums: the Magritte Museum, which forms part of the Fine Arts Museum, and the René Magritte Museum, located in his former house.

Magritte liked to tell people he wasn't a surrealist. "I just paint Belgium as I see it," he explained, mysteriously. He grew up in the grim industrial suburbs of Charleroi and once claimed his earliest memory was a hot air balloon landing on his pram. His mother's suicide brought sadness to his childhood.

The mystery of Magritte is reflected in the apartment where he lived with Georgette from 1924 to 1954. It was acquired by two art dealers, who carefully refurnished it in Magritte's unsettling style.

He painted some of his most famous works in this apartment. Sometimes he included a detail of his house. The fireplace in the sitting room appears in his painting *La Durée poignardeé*, where a steam train emerges from a wall; the double doors leading to the bedroom turn up in the sinister painting of a giant boulder titled *Le Monde Invisible*.

No one is more Belgian than Magritte. He might look like a dull bank clerk, but the dullness is a disguise. He is actually a revolutionary, plotting to turn the world on its head.

VAN EYCK ALTARPIECE

The Van Eyck Altarpiece in Ghent Cathedral is one of the greatest paintings of the Middle Ages. It is an astonishing work, painted on 24 wood panels, filled with endless fascinating details.

The altarpiece was probably begun by Hubert van Eyck in the 1420s, and completed after his death in 1425 by his younger brother Jan, whose modest motto was: *"Als ik kan"* (If I can).

Yes, he could, you might argue. Completed in 1432, the altarpiece was a shockingly original work that included the first realistic nudes in painting. Van Eyck also painted the earliest cityscapes, the most realistic mirrors, the most convincing fountains, and the most accurate botanical paintings of flowers and trees.

But this massive altarpiece became the most endangered work of art in history. It was hidden during the 16th-century religious wars, plundered by Napoleon, hidden again during the First World War and stolen by the Nazis in the Second World War.

Yet the altarpiece has miraculously survived virtually intact. Recovered in 1945, it now hangs in Ghent Cathedral, close to the chapel where it was unveiled in 1432, with just one panel still missing after it was stolen in 1934.

It is one of the great achievements of European art that you should try to see. But if you can't get to Ghent, you can examine the painting online in astonishing detail.

Heron
Bastionstraat 13
Ghent

Rabbit
—
Tempelhof 36
Ghent
—
209 Hackney Road
London

ROA

His colossal sleeping animals can be seen on walls all over the world, but Belgian street artist ROA remains an enigma. Born in 1976, he started out in mellow, tolerant Ghent. His beautifully drawn sleeping rabbits and dead birds appeared on side walls and abandoned buildings across the Flemish city, including a group of four sleeping rabbits on a wall at Tempelhof 36.

The drawings were done in a simple palette of black, white and grey. His technique was inspired by Old Masters like Rembrandt. But he chose to do his work on abandoned walls where he sometimes used a drainpipe or ledge as part of the composition.

ROA's art can be spotted on buildings across the world, from London to New York City. They have become landmarks loved by locals, tourists and fellow street artists. When a council in East London threatened in 2010 to paint over a rabbit on the side of a recording studio, fans launched an online campaign that finally saved the work.

More recently, ROA has become a hero of the environmental movement with his precise drawings of endangered animals in urban settings. He is probably Belgium's most famous contemporary artist, even if no one knows his name.

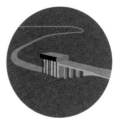

ICONIC
buildings

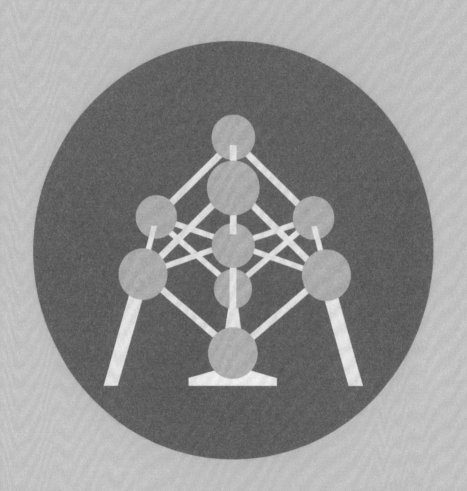

Atomium
Square de l'Atomium 1
Laeken
+32 (0)2 475 47 75
atomium.be

ATOMIUM

Built in 1958 for the Brussels World Fair, the Atomium is one of the world's strangest buildings. It was designed by the engineer André Waterkeyn, who had originally proposed an inverted Eiffel Tower. After that idea was rejected, he went back to the drawing board and designed a giant steel structure modelled on an iron atom magnified 165 billion times.

An optimistic symbol of the atomic age, the 102-metre structure consists of nine large spheres connected by 20 long metal tubes. It incorporates a high-speed lift, an observation deck and a panoramic restaurant.

One of the last relics of Expo 58, the Atomium was meant to be a temporary structure. Yet Belgians have become attached to this eccentric, oddly cool structure. Restored in 2006, it is now the most popular tourist attraction in Brussels.

One of the nine spheres contains an exhibition dedicated to Expo 58, while a further three are used for temporary exhibitions. But the most surprising sphere has been turned into a dorm where kids can spend the night in small coloured pods designed by the Spanish artist Alicia Framis.

The building is best seen at night when the steel spheres are lit by three thousand tiny lights, like an alien spaceship that has landed on the edge of the Belgian capital. It is now one of the last relics of an optimistic age.

Horta Museum
Rue Américaine 25
Saint-Gilles
+32 (0)2 543 04 90
hortamuseum.be

Maison Autrique
Chaussée de Haecht 266
Schaerbeek
+32 (0)2 215 66 00
autrique.be

ART NOUVEAU HOUSES

The streets of Belgian cities are dotted with exceptional buildings in art nouveau style. You come upon them by chance while wandering down a quiet street in Brussels, Liège or Antwerp. Some of the buildings have become dilapidated over the years. Others have been lovingly restored.

The art nouveau style was mainly developed in Brussels by architects such as Victor Horta and Paul Hankar. They created fabulous buildings for wealthy clients in an exotic style that used glass, iron and stone in a flowing style inspired by organic forms.

More than one thousand art nouveau buildings were constructed in Brussels between 1894 and 1914, but many have been torn down, leaving about 500 still standing. Many are privately owned, so you can only admire the details on the façade. But a small number can be visited, including the Horta Museum, the Maison Autrique, the Old England department store and the Maison Saint-Cyr.

Several neighbourhoods in Brussels have large clusters of art nouveau houses, including the St Boniface quarter, the Square Ambiorix and the Ixelles ponds neighbourhoods. But perhaps the most surprising concentration is found in Rue Vanderschrick in Saint-Gilles where architect Ernest Blerot designed a row of 14 art nouveau houses in different styles.

Victor Horta finally abandoned the style he had helped to create. No one could afford art nouveau in the years after the First World War and his final works were large public buildings in a sober modern style, including Gare Centrale in Brussels and the Palais des Beaux-Arts – now BOZAR.

		Frituur Davy	**Chez Clémentine**
		AT: Bissegem station	Place de Saint-Job 40
		Vlaswaagplein	Uccle
		Bissegem	+32 (0)483 57 75 23
		frituurdavy.be	*chezclem.be*

FRIETKOTEN

Belgium often appears a deeply divided country, but the *frietkot*, or *baraque à frites*, is one of the few places that still bring people together. It's an essential part of the national culture, like the royal family or the cobbled roads. You find these shacks on town squares, outside railway stations and on the old N highways. Every Belgian has a favourite. It might be Frituur Davy, outside the train station in Bissegem, or Chez Clémentine in the chic Brussels suburb of Uccle.

They are normally simple structures. Nothing fancy. They will have a counter, a canopy to keep off the rain and maybe a few plastic chairs scattered around outside.

Sometimes they are built of wood, sometimes aluminium. The more ambitious examples might be designed to look like Alpine chalets. But often the fries shack is nothing more than an old touring caravan parked by the side of the road.

Like the *currywurst* stands in Berlin, or the hot dog sellers in Stockholm, the fries stands serve a basic need for comfort food. At night, they glow with warm fluorescent light, like a painting by Edward Hopper. You shelter under the canopy along with the other lonely nighthawks, chat about the weather, share stories.

You don't always eat at a *frietkot*, but sometimes it is just what you need. Nowhere else offers that unique mix of warmth, conversation and comfort food.

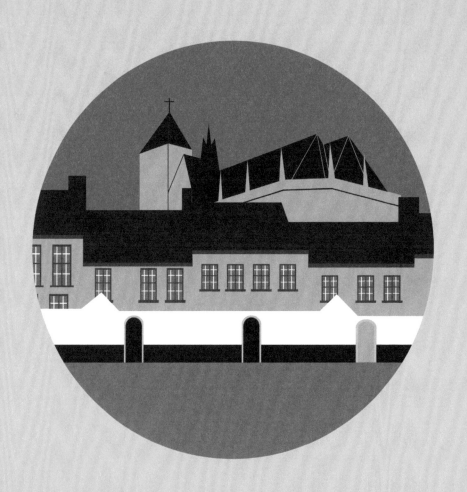

BEGUINAGES

Beguinages (*begijnhoven* in Dutch) are often hidden behind high walls. It isn't always easy to find the entrance. But that is what makes these places so special.

You can find beguinages in most of the large towns of northern Belgium. These silent walled communities date back to the Middle Ages when they were occupied by single women. The beguines who lived there were religious, but not too saintly. They had their own houses with neat little gardens concealed behind high walls.

The Beguine movement began in the 12th century after the Crusades had killed off a large percentage of young men in northern Europe. Founded by a priest – Lambert le Bègue – in Liège, the movement spread through the Low Countries, northern France and Germany, but it was concentrated in Belgium, which once had 94 beguinages. There are now just 26, including 13 listed as UNESCO World Heritage sites.

Each beguinage follows a different pattern. The beguinage in Bruges is a large complex of whitewashed houses overlooking a green space planted with trees. It is beautiful in spring, when thousands of daffodils appear. But it can get overcrowded. And, despite notices calling for silence, it is not very peaceful.

The beguinage in Mechelen has lost its walls, leaving just a warren of cobbled lanes around an old brewery. The Klein Begijnhof in Ghent is like a secret walled village next to a busy road.

Antwerp's Begijnhof stands on the edge of the busy university quarter, yet almost no one comes here. You could live in Antwerp for years without ever entering the little door at Rodestraat 39. It leads past an empty porter's lodge into a secret garden surrounded by neat 16th-century brick houses.

There are other beguinages in the historic towns of Kortrijk, Diest and Lier. There is even a tiny beguinage in the Brussels suburb of Anderlecht. Each one feels like a secret village in the heart of a city.

ISOLATED TOWN HOUSES

The Belgian landscape is dotted with mysterious isolated houses. They look like the narrow terraced houses painted by Magritte. But these buildings stand alone in the middle of nowhere, as if a town was planned, but abandoned after one house. It makes no sense. This is Belgium at its strangest.

The narrow houses all share a similar design. They are built of brick, two or three stories in height, rather modestly decorated. The side walls have no windows. They are known in Flanders as *wachtmuren*, or waiting walls. Sometimes they are covered with grey insulation panels to protect the brick walls. Sometimes they have signs advertising supermarkets or cars.

The lonely town houses mostly date from the early 20th century when local regulations allowed families with limited funds to build houses on narrow plots of farmland. The owners chose an incongruous urban style of architecture for their isolated houses, rather than a more rural style.

Maybe they were hoping that others would join them. But it never happened. One hundred years on, the houses still look as if they belong in a crowded city. Not in the middle of a field.

City Hall Bruges
Burg 12
Bruges
museabrugge.be

City Hall Brussels
Grand-Place 1
Brussels
brussels.be

TOWN HALLS

Belgians like to claim they are modest. Not like, let's say, the French or the Dutch. But they have built some spectacular town halls. Known as the *Stadhuis* in Flanders, or the *Hôtel de Ville* in Wallonia, these municipal buildings often resemble royal palaces. But they are just places to register the birth of a child or pay a parking fine.

Many of the most impressive town halls date from the Middle Ages, when cities in this region of Europe were emerging as centres of power and wealth. The town hall was more than a building; it was a municipal branding exercise.

The exceptionally ornate Stadhuis in Bruges provided the model for other cities to follow. Begun in 1376, this sublime Gothic building was completed in 1421. Its façade is decorated with rows of statues representing powerful figures in the city's history.

The town hall in Bruges was still being built when two architects started work on a new town hall on the market square in Brussels. Begun in 1402, it was clearly inspired by the Gothic style of Bruges. It has the same architectural details, such as turrets and pointed arches, the same rows of statues.

The town hall in Antwerp was built in a new style for a new age. Designed by the architect Cornelis Floris De Vriendt, it follows the architectural rules of the Italian Renaissance. It was much easier to build than the fanciful Gothic structures. Begun in 1561, it took just four years to complete.

As Belgian cities expanded in the 19th century, impressive new town halls were built in the suburbs. The Brussels municipality of Saint-Gilles built a magnificent town hall inspired by the castles of the Loire.

Most Belgians only visit the town hall when they have a bill to pay or a document to be stamped. Some annoying administrative task that has to be done. But they often do it in a spectacular building.

UGLY BELGIAN HOUSES

Belgians like to be different. But sometimes they go too far. They buy a plot of land in the suburbs, find an architect and build the house of their dreams.

It might be a replica of a French château, or something that is meant to look like an old Flemish farmhouse, or perhaps the inspiration was a Chinese temple. It seems anything is possible in the Belgian suburbs.

Some people shrug their shoulders. This is Belgium, after all. But blogger Hannes Coudenys from West Flanders was offended by the houses he saw as he cycled down the road to work. He created a site on Facebook called 'Ugly Belgian Houses'.

Hannes would photograph an ugly house and add a cheeky caption in his 'ugly Belgian English', like "Why is this house wearing a snorkel mask?" or "Was your architect called Frank Lloyd Wrong?" The project turned into a book, an exhibition and a national obsession.

Some people were upset because they discovered their house was in the book. They would try to argue their house wasn't ugly. It was just different from the neighbours. Interesting, you might say.

And then one day Coudenys changed his mind. In a television interview, he said he was sorry. He was wrong about the ugly houses. They might be ugly, but they make Belgium unique.

BELFRIES

In a country that prides itself on its modesty, the belfries seem out of place. Dating from the Middle Ages, these soaring towers rise above the flat landscape as symbols of urban wealth and civic pride.

The belfry originally contained the bells that were used to mark the time, festivals and church services, as well as alerting the city to fires and attacks. It was also used as a storehouse for the city's treasury and archives.

"In the market-place of Bruges stands the belfry old and brown," begins the famous poem *The Belfry of Bruges* by Henry Longfellow. Begun in about 1240, the belfry in Bruges was one of the first to be built. It has a distinctive octagonal top added in the 1480s to bring the height to 83 metres. The observation platform at the top is reached by a steep, narrow staircase of 366 stone steps, now heavily worn.

The town of Ghent proved it could beat its rival Bruges when it began work on its belfry in 1313. The tower was finally completed in 1380 when a gilded dragon was placed on top.

Rising 95 metres above the flat plains, it is the tallest belfry in Belgium, some eight metres higher than Bruges. And that's not all. The city added a modern lift to eliminate the stiff climb to the top.

Boat lift of Strépy-Thieu
Rue Raymond Cordier 50
Thieu
canalducentre.be

USELESS PROJECTS

Most Belgians can tell you about a bridge leading nowhere, an unused motorway or some other useless structure near their home. Many were built in the 1980s when the Belgian government adopted a policy to balance regional development. It meant that any big infrastructure in one language region had to be matched by an equally large infrastructure in the other region, even if it was totally unnecessary.

Eventually someone found a word to describe this policy. They came up with the term *wafelijzerpolitiek*, or *la politique du gaufrier*, which means, literally, waffle iron policy.

This led to bridges being built in the middle of nowhere, ghost metro stations in Antwerp and Charleroi, and ports that ships never visited. The biggest folly is the funicular boat lift at Strépy-Thieu, a massive structure that is hardly ever used, except by tourist boats.

A Belgian journalist suggested the concept of 'Grands Travaux Inutiles', or Major Useless Projects, to describe these unique Belgian structures. A campaign was launched in 2008 to come up with creative uses for these useless structures. But then the government started spending large sums tearing down the grand useless projects.

ICONIC
brands

brands

Sint-Sixtus Abbey
Donkerstraat 12
Westvleteren
trappistwestvleteren.be

In de Vrede
Donkerstraat 13
Westvleteren
+32 (0)57 40 03 77
indevrede.be

WESTVLETEREN 12

Westvleteren 12 is frequently ranked as the world's best beer. It is definitely one of the hardest to find. The 19 Trappist monks of Sint-Sixtus Abbey, 12 km from Poperinge, brew barely more than 5000 barrels of Westvleteren every year. It is almost impossible to find anywhere except the abbey shop and the cafe outside the gates.

Everything about this dark brown beer is mysterious, from the glass bottles with no labels to the wooden crates with the name Westvleteren stencilled on the side. The monks brew three versions of Westvleteren Trappist beers: Blond, 8 and 12. The Westvleteren 12 is the strongest of the three at just over 10% alcohol.

The monks who brewed Westvleteren used to lead a quiet life, selling a few crates of beer to occasional visitors. But in 2005 the website *ratebeer.com* ranked Westvleteren 12 the best beer in the world and suddenly the peaceful religious retreat was mobbed by beer fans from all over the world.

As soon as Westvleteren hit the top ranking, it became almost impossible to get hold of a crate. The phone line was always busy and a long queue of cars blocked all the roads around the abbey.

Yet the monks refused to change their principles. They continued to brew relatively modest amounts on four days a month. Enough to support the abbey, no more than that, whereas the Trappist monks at Orval produce ten times as much every year.

It all changed in 2019 when the Sint-Sixtus monks discovered a supermarket was cheating the system by selling bottles of Westvleteren at more than twice the cost price. Now the monks have gone digital and set up a website where private individuals can order three crates of 24 bottles.

Or you can simply call in at In de Vrede, the abbey cafe, and order a glass of Westvleteren 12 along with a plate of Westvleteren pâté. You might almost be in heaven.

DECAP DANCE ORGANS

Head down on a Sunday afternoon to the small corner bar called Cafe Beveren on the Scheldt waterfront in Antwerp. If you are lucky, you'll hear one of the last authentic Decap dance organs in the world.

Dance organs were immensely popular in Antwerp in the first half of the 20th century. These huge mechanical instruments replaced live orchestras in almost every dance hall in town. Meanwhile, smaller, quieter versions were manufactured for local bars, where romantic couples would while away an afternoon drinking beer and waltzing to the music.

Most cafes got rid of their Decap organs in the 1960s when juke boxes came along and dancing couples migrated to discotheques. Some have been preserved in museums, like the glorious Decap organ in Utrecht's Museum Speelklok.

The Gebroeders Decap (Decap Brothers) still have a workshop in Antwerp hidden behind a grey garage door. They mainly repair one or two old models that have survived and rent out their own Decap organ.

The beautiful art deco dance organ in Cafe Beveren was made by the Gebroeders Decap in 1937. Incorporating an accordion, drums and a saxophone, the organ blasts out nostalgic melodies during the weekend that shake the beer glasses behind the bar.

Le 27
Boulevard de Waterloo 27
Brussels
+32 (0)2 513 05 02
delvaux.com

DELVAUX

Delvaux is a discreet company. You may never have heard the name. It doesn't shout. Yet Delvaux is the world's oldest luxury goods company. Older than Vuitton or Hermès. But discreet. Belgian.

Founded in 1829 by Charles Delvaux, the company began producing elegant handmade trunks for wealthy European travellers and later specialised in luxury leather goods. When it filed a patent for a small woman's bag in 1908, the company essentially invented the modern handbag. Its team of 45 craftsmen currently produce about 15.000 luxury handbags a year in a Brussels workshop based in a former army barracks.

Its most successful line is the Brillant bag designed by the Belgian architect Paule Goethals. Launched in 1958 for the Brussels World Fair, it was branded with a buckle in the shape of a D. Other companies went on to imitate this innovative idea, like Chanel with its double C.

Delvaux now has more than 40 boutiques across the world, each a unique design, including a landmark shop on Fifth Avenue in New York decorated with old leather cutting tools and a chandelier from a Belgian church. But its home is still in Brussels. Discreetly hidden.

TOMORROWLAND

Belgium has a lot of cool music festivals, like Werchter in Flanders and Dour in Wallonia. But Tomorrowland is unique. Staged in the sleepy Flemish town of Boom, near Antwerp, it is the world's most popular electronic dance festival.

Tomorrowland attracts more than 400.000 people from as far off as Australia and China. Some arrive on a special Tomorrowland-themed Brussels Airlines plane with dance music playing as soon as the plane is in the air.

Launched in 2005 by the brothers Manu and Michiel Beers, the festival took a few years to become established. But word finally got out about its lavish stage designs, gourmet restaurants and relaxed mood. Tickets now sell out within a few hours of going online.

The brothers still run the festival themselves from their smart Tomorrowland HQ building in Antwerp, designed by Dieter vander Velpen Architects. They have gone on to launch spin-off festivals in the United States and Brazil, along with a winter festival in the Alps. The company employs a permanent staff of 80, along with a crew of 12.000 during the festival, which is estimated to contribute more than 100 million euro to the Belgian economy.

"It's beyond a festival," explained the Dutch DJ Armin van Buuren. "It's a music festival combined with a theme park combined with a food festival combined with a cultural event."

SMURFS

The Smurfs *(Les Schtroumpfs* in French) were invented by the illustrator Pierre Culliford in 1958. He was dining with a fellow cartoonist at the Belgian coast and, unable to remember the word for salt cellar, he asked his friend to pass the *schtroumpf.*

The Smurfs were little blue figures who lived in mushroom-shaped houses in the forest. Culliford (who signed himself Peyo) developed more than 100 different characters with cute names corresponding to their personalities, like Disney's seven dwarfs, so you have Brainy Smurf, who wears glasses but isn't all that smart, Greedy Smurf, who is seldom seen without a cake, and Smurfette, who was originally the only female in the Smurf village.

The Smurfs developed into a global brand, with books, figures, sweets, theme parks, video games and even a Smurf Song that reached No. 1 in 16 countries in 1978.

Peyo's little figures spoke a baffling language in which words were often replaced by 'smurf', so you might get someone saying: "I'm smurfing off to the smurf".

Their fame spread in the 1980s when Smurf cartoons were shown on children's TV, followed by several full-length movies. In 2018, Brussels Airlines decorated an Airbus plane with the Smurfs.

Some critics have seen these innocent figures as secretly representing political ideas. "Could the Smurf village be a communist utopia?" a leading American newspaper asked. Most Belgians would argue it is just a simple story of smurfing Smurfs.

Stella Artois brewery
Aarschotsesteenweg 20
Leuven
breweryvisits.com

STELLA ARTOIS

Stella Artois is an average Belgian lager that you might drink in a station bar before catching the train home. It's not really all that special, but it is marketed in Britain and America as a sophisticated French beer.

Stella Artois has always been a confusing brand. It was first brewed in 1926 in the Artois brewery in the Flemish university town of Leuven. Yet the label on the bottle gives the date 1366.

The company traces its origins back to a tiny brewery called Den Hoorn (The Horn) that was mentioned in the Leuven city records in 1366. The brewery grew rapidly after 1425 when Leuven university was founded. The name changed to Artois when master brewer Sébastien Artois bought the brewery in 1717. And the name Stella (star) was added to the beer in 1926.

When Stella Artois was launched in the United Kingdom in 1976, it was branded a 'premium lager' and served in its own distinctive glass. "Reassuringly expensive," the slogan defiantly claimed. The beer was marketed in a series of lavish adverts modelled on new wave French movies, and so everyone thought the beer from Leuven was a sophisticated French drink that might fit in well with an evening at an arty cinema watching Jean-Luc Godard.

The brand hit an image problem when it emerged that the strong Belgian lager was linked to binge drinking. It was suddenly no longer a chic French beer but 'a wife beater'. The brewery finally decided to reduce the alcohol content to save its reputation.

Overlooking the canal Leuvense Vaart, the Stella Artois brewery is now part of the giant beer multinational AB InBev, with headquarters in Brazil.

The company tried in 2010 to persuade local people in Leuven that Stella was a premium lager. But no one was fooled. It was just a refreshing beer that they liked to drink in their local bar. Reassuringly Belgian, you might want to say.

Natan-Couture
Avenue Louise 158
Ixelles
+32 (0)2 647 10 01

Atelier II
Place Georges
Brugmann 6
Ixelles
natan.be

NATAN

The fashion brand Natan has occupied the same grand town house on Avenue Louise since 1930. Founded by Paul Natan, it was taken over in 1984 by the young interior designer Edouard Vermeulen from Ypres. He developed a distinctive style based on strong colours, flowing fabrics and perfect needlework.

His beautiful dresses caught the attention of Belgian royalty and celebrities. He designed the wedding dress worn by Princess Mathilde in 1999, and Justine Henin's wedding dress in 2015. He also designed the red dress worn by Princess Máxima when she married the future Dutch king Willem-Alexander.

In 2017, Vermeulen opened an artist's studio on the first floor of his shop on Rue de Namur in Brussels where he exhibits clothes by young Belgian designers. The following year, he unveiled a workshop – Atelier II – on the elegant Place Georges Brugmann where customers can observe seamstresses creating Natan dresses in elegant white rooms.

ATOMA

Every Belgian schoolkid has a bag full of Atoma notebooks. These distinctive A4 and A5 notebooks come with 144 perforated pages protected by corrugated cardboard or plastic covers. But the truly unique feature is the binding system consisting of a row of 11 independent plastic discs that hold the pages in place, making it easy to move pages around.

The disc-binding system was designed in 1948 by the French inventors André Tomas and André Martin (whose initials gave the brand its name). They created the notebooks for the Brussels stationery company Papeteries Mottart. A huge success in Belgium, they were for many years compulsory in schools.

The notebooks are now produced in a factory in Dilbeek, outside Brussels. More than one million are sold every year, mainly in the busy days before school starts in September. A limited number are sold in Germany, Japan and Scandinavia as luxury items. The family firm has also launched special editions created by Belgian designers such as Alain Berteau and Luc Vincent.

The patent has now lapsed, so competitors can introduce rival notebooks. The company has had to cut back staff. But Atoma remains a family business with a unique product. Brilliant, but a little weird. Like Belgium, you might argue.

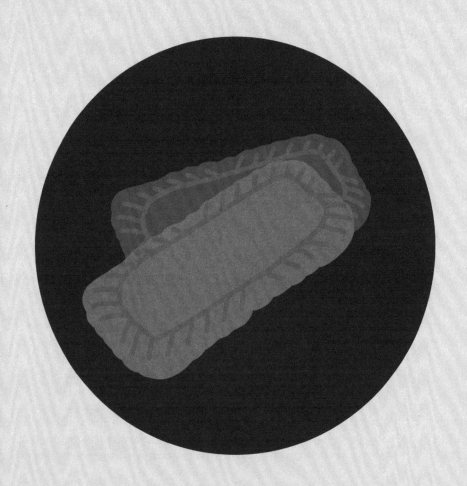

LOTUS

You can complain about the grey skies or the insane traffic, but you cannot fault the way they serve coffee in Belgium. You just ask for a coffee, and the waiter nods, and brings you a coffee on a silver or wooden tray, along with a sachet of sugar, a little pot of milk and a Lotus speculoos biscuit.

These distinctive biscuits in their red wrappers have been baked in the small Belgian town of Lembeke since 1932, when Jan Boone developed a recipe based on the traditional Flemish ginger-bread biscuits given to children on *Sinterklaas* (St Nicholas Day), 6 December.

Boone and his brother went on to expand the business by selling the biscuits from a red truck. In the 1950s, they came up with the idea of selling individually wrapped biscuits to cafes to serve with coffee. The idea spread to France and the Netherlands. They are served in train stations, hotels and on planes. The family business now produces some six billion biscuits every year, along with Lotus paste and ice cream.

With their unique blend of cinnamon, ginger and nutmeg, the little biscuits from Lembeke went on to conquer America in the 1980s. Renamed Lotus Biscoff cookies, they were branded 'Europe's favourite cookie with coffee' and served on many American flights.

When United Airlines announced in 2020 that they were replacing Lotus Biscoff with Oreo Thins, passengers posted angry messages online, forcing the airline to abandon its plans.

ICONIC
curiosities

MADAME PIPI

People always complain. Why do we have to pay 50 cents to use a public toilet in a train station, a cafe or a nightclub? The charge is usually collected by a strict woman who sits at a small table near the entrance. They call her Madame Pipi.

It's not a glamorous job. Madame Pipi has to spend the day in a dim underground toilet dealing with annoying customers. Someone will claim to have no change. A mother will ask if her children can get in free. A tourist will be baffled by it all.

Madame Pipi doesn't wear a uniform. But there is an unofficial dress code. She wears comfortable shoes, a cheap patterned dress and an apron that can be easily cleaned. She sits at a small round table covered with a plastic cloth, a comfortable chair, a cheap fan, and maybe a vase of flowers. To pass the time, she might read a gossip magazine.

Madame Pipi has everything she needs for the job – a yellow bucket, a mop, a cloth and a range of strong cleaning products. She often favours a cleaning brand called Mr. Propre. Mr Clean. They make a formidable couple, Madame Pipi and Monsieur Propre.

She will put out a white saucer to collect the coins. Attached to the wall, a handwritten sign, in two languages, French and Dutch. *Service €0,50 Dienst*, it might say. *Merci Dank U*. Occasionally, it will be in English as well, for the foreign customers.

But it's a hard life. The women – they are almost always women – rely on tips to provide a modest income. Many use it to supplement their pension. They often have to pay for the equipment themselves and perhaps also a small rent.

It might not seem an exciting job. Except sometimes it can be. Cristina Cerquiera worked for many years in the toilets of the Beursschouwburg theatre in Brussels. Annoyed at the many customers who didn't pay, she decided to let people leave a drawing as payment. After ten years, she had 250 notebooks filled with sketches. In 2019, the theatre organised an exhibition based on the notebooks.

194

**Belgian Comic
Strip Center**
Rue des Sables 20
Brussels
+32 (0)2 219 19 80
comicscenter.net

Mural Le Jeune Albert
By: Yves Chaland
Rue des Alexiens 49
Brussels

COMIC BOOKS

Here's one thing that unites Belgium. Everyone reads comic books. Not just children. Everyone loves to read the illustrated books featuring characters like Lucky Luke, Spirou or Tintin.

No other country is so addicted to this form of fantasy fiction. People in Belgium have been devouring comic books since the 1930s. Every Belgian house has a stack of old Tintin books and maybe a few contemporary comic books as well. Some of the older comic illustrators may have died, but this small country still has more than 700 artists working on comic books.

You find specialised comic bookshops all over Belgium, often in quiet back streets. Maybe not as many as before, but it's still an important industry in Belgium, with some 40 million comic books produced every year.

The Belgian Comic Strip Center opened in 1989 in an abandoned art nouveau department store in Brussels. The building lies down a dingy street where you would hardly expect to find one of the country's most inspiring museums.

In 1991, the city of Brussels started to decorate the dull grey walls of downtown buildings with large cartoon murals based on classic comic books. More than 50 walls have now been decorated in the style of comic book illustrators, like the Yves Chaland wall, which shows a typical Brussels street scene in the 1950s.

FRONT GARDENS

Belgians don't like to conform. Every house in a street is different. And every front garden is unique. You might see a garden where every hint of green has been stripped away. Or a garden with a sad palm tree that has died in the cold Belgian weather.

Some front gardens are miniature works of art. Belgians are eclectic in their tastes. Their ideas often come from other countries and other periods. You might see a garden laid out in the strict formal style of the Italian Renaissance, while the neighbour next door has modelled their small space on English landscape style.

There are elegant gardens with boxwood hedges and topiary trees that have been carefully clipped to create perfect shapes. And there are also front gardens filled with garden gnomes.

But of course some Belgian gardens are small. The owners have to make do with a tiny plot of land to achieve an impressive effect. It doesn't always work out, but some gardens are miniature masterpieces.

Rue de l'Étuve
Brussels
manneken-pis.com

MANNEKEN PIS

Everyone who visits Belgium knows they have to look at a statue in Brussels called *Manneken Pis*. And everyone is disappointed when they see it. It's tiny (55,5 cm). It's ridiculous. And yet this little statue on a street corner is the national symbol.

The Manneken Pis represents a small naked boy urinating into a stone basin. The original dates from the middle of the 15th century. It was replaced in about 1620 by a bronze copy designed by the baroque sculptor Jérôme Duquesnoy the Elder. The replica survived the bombardment of Brussels in 1695 and became a symbol of the city. It has been stolen several times. Once, in 1745, it was recovered in Geraardsbergen. The city of Brussels presented Geraardsbergen with a copy to show their gratitude.

One of the city's most eccentric traditions is to create elaborate costumes for the Manneken Pis. It started when Louis XIV presented the Manneken with a miniature uniform. The custom became extremely popular after the Second World War when hundreds of costumes were presented, ranging from Dracula to Elvis. Anyone can submit a design to the mayor of Brussels who passes on the proposal to the Order of the Manneken Pis. More than 1000 tiny costumes are stored in a town house known as the *Garderobe* or *Kleedkamer* (Wardrobe).

The souvenir shops in the neighbourhood sell ridiculous replicas, including beer dispensers, corkscrews and garden fountains. Not everyone approves the naked boy. In the Brussels version of Monopoly released in 2019, the figure of Manneken Pis is dressed in a pair of swimming trunks.

It might seem ridiculous, but the Manneken Pis has become a symbol of Belgium. It reflects the country's endless appetite for earthy humour, self-mockery and frivolous fun. Nothing else would do.

RAIN

It always rains in Belgium. No point planning a barbeque or a summer wedding. And never forget to take an umbrella. It always rains, they say, especially on the National Day, 21 July, when the King and Queen inspect the army, concerts are organised and parents take their kids to the beach. Why bother when it always rains on Belgian National Day? They even have a term for it. The *drache nationale*, or national downpour.

But does it really? The Belgian weatherman Frank Deboosere looked at the figures. He concluded that rainfall in Belgium wasn't exceptional, but that it rained a little on most days. He also bust the myth of the national downpour by studying the weather over 140 years. It turned out that 73 national days have been dry and only ten experienced a downpour of more than 10 mm, according to Deboosere. Maybe you can risk going out without an umbrella after all.

COBBLESTONES

They can be annoying, especially for cyclists, but Belgian cobbled roads have a certain charm. They go back to a time when travel was slow, and difficult, and sometimes dangerous.

Some cobbled roads run through ancient forests. Others lead to mediaeval castles. Sometimes called *kinderkoppen* – children's heads – the cobbles are an essential part of the Belgian landscape. They make it harder to get anywhere, but the journey is always interesting.

The cobblestoned streets in Brussels are among the most beautiful in the world. After years of indifference, the city is now preserving this aspect of its heritage. The type of cobblestone varies from one neighbourhood to the next. The hard grey stones laid out on Grand-Place are made from Belgian granite quarried in Wallonia. Just a few streets away, Place Saint-Jean is paved with light grey Belgian sandstone. The lovely sloping Rue des Renards in the Marolles features a warm red cobblestone mined near Jodoigne. Other streets are laid with imported sandstone cobbles from Portugal, India or China.

The old city of Bruges has kept almost all its cobbled streets. The elegant grey stones give the city a warm and aged feel. They also slow down traffic in the old town centre. Cyclists and even pedestrians complain about the uncomfortable surfaces, but cobbles are part of the national identity.

Brasserie Cantillon
Rue Gheude 56
Anderlecht
+32 (0)2 521 49 28
cantillon.be

**Brouwerij
Drie Fonteinen**
Molenstraat 47
Lot (Beersel)
+32 (0)2 306 71 03
3fonteinen.be

GUEUZE

In the quiet villages of the Pajottenland hills, something strange is brewing. The air is filled with wild yeasts and microbes that cause spontaneous fermentation. The microbes react with a liquid wort made from malted barley that sits in open tanks. On cold nights, the yeasts turn the wort into a beer known as lambic.

The raw lambic is aged in oak barrels for at least three years to create the more complex Gueuze beers. Sometimes local cherries are added to create the sweet red beer known as Kriek.

It's a unique beer. The particular microbes are only found in a small geographical area near Brussels. The breweries are strung out along the valley of the River Zenne to the west of Brussels. The owners often run guided tours at weekends, or there might be a cafe next door where you can try out the beers.

It used to be difficult to find Gueuze and Lambic beers in Belgium. It was a niche taste. Only a handful of cafes stocked it in Brussels. It was easier to buy it in Helsinki or Boston.

Then something happened. Belgians started to appreciate the sour taste of an authentic Gueuze like Cantillon. Young brewers took over some of the old Gueuze breweries outside Brussels, like Brouwerij Drie Fonteinen, and Belgian cafes began to sell these rather peculiar beers. Now it is cool to drink a Gueuze. Even if no one likes the taste at first.

ICONIC
ideas &
inventions

La Maison de
Monsieur Sax
Rue Adolphe Sax 37
Dinant
sax.dinant.be/
sax-and-the-city

**Musical Instruments
Museum**
Montagne de la Cour 2
Brussels
+32 (0)2 545 01 30
mim.be

SAXOPHONE

The inventor of the saxophone, Adolphe Sax, came from the modest river town of Dinant in the Ardennes. The town proudly celebrates its most famous son with 12 painted saxophones on the bridge across the River Meuse, along with a Sax fountain, Sax music kiosk and a small museum on the site of the house where he was born in 1814.

It might strike you as overblown, but Dinant doesn't think so. It sells itself to tourists with the slogan: 'Sax and the City'. And celebrates the saxophone in a small, quirky museum filled with contorted brass instruments that blast out saxophone recordings at the push of a button.

The inventor didn't stay that many years in Dinant. He left in his teens, studied music in Brussels, and worked for a time in his father's instrument workshop. He built the first saxophone in 1841 and performed it for the first time in Brussels.

Sax moved to Paris the following year to promote his instrument, which was praised by Berlioz. He set up a large workshop in the French capital and in 1846 filed 14 patents for a range of saxophones.

The new instrument became popular with French army bands and was later adopted by composers such as Bizet and Ravel. It crossed the Atlantic as a brass band instrument and was taken up in the 1920s by New Orleans jazz bands and solo performers such as Charlie Parker and John Coltrane.

In 1992, Bill Clinton celebrated his victory in the Democratic nomination for president by playing *Heartbreak Hotel* on his tenor saxophone. Two years later, Clinton travelled to Brussels to meet European leaders. He didn't visit Dinant, although he was invited. But he began his speech with a word of thanks to Sax. "I have a great personal debt of nearly 40 years' standing to this country," he declared, "because it was a Belgian, Adolphe Sax, who invented the saxophone."

ideas &	**Arizona**	**Fietsen Cattrysse**
inventions	Zeedijk 37	Leopoldlaan 16
	De Panne	De Haan
	+32 (0)478 22 28 10	+32 (0)59 23 43 77
	+32 (0)58 41 16 92	*cattrysse.be*
	arizona-depanne.be	

CUISTAX

You see them in all the resorts along the coast. They look like large pedal cars made for adults. They are called cuistax from the French words *cuisse*, a bottom, and *tax*, short for taxi. The Flemish call them *billenkarren,* or bum cars.

They come in all sizes. The smallest versions can take one child. Larger vehicles can carry four people. Even larger ones are big enough to transport a family of four, two grandparents and a dog. And occasionally an enormous cuistax will roll along the promenade with a dozen people on board.

The cuistax craze started in 1936 when a bicycle manufacturer in the little town of Zedelgem came up with the idea of welding two bikes together and bolting a plank between them. The invention caught on in the 1960s as Belgians flocked to the beaches. One of the oldest family firms, Arizona in the seaside town of De Panne, was founded more than 60 years ago.

Occasionally, they are involved in accidents. Sometimes serious. But no seaside town would dream of banning the cuistax. They are an essential element of the Belgian summer, part of the fun, along with waffles and minigolf.

*ideas &
inventions*

Design Museum Gent
Jan Breydelstraat 5
Ghent
+32 (0)9 267 99 99
designmuseumgent.be
—
maartenvanseveren.be
vitra.com

.03 CHAIR

In 2010 Design Museum Gent devoted an entire exhibition to a single chair by the Belgian designer Maarten Van Severen. Known as the .03, the chair is considered a masterpiece of modern design.

Born in 1956, Van Severen came from an artistic family. After studying architecture at Sint-Lucas in Ghent, he set out to create the perfect chair. Working from first principles, he produced several timeless designs.

Most chairs consist of several elements, but the .03 is a simple streamlined shape. Mass produced since 1998 by the Vitra company, the chair is found in locations across the world, including Seattle public library, the Centre Pompidou in Paris and Filigranes bookshop in Brussels.

Van Severen's chair can also be spotted in several places in Ghent, including Design Museum Gent, Ghent Cathedral and the university library.

Mercatormuseum
Zamanstraat 49-D
Sint-Niklaas
+32 (0)3 778 34 50
musea.sint-niklaas.be/
mercator

MERCATOR PROJECTION

The Belgian cartographer Gerard Mercator shaped the modern view of the world with his map drawn in 1569. He set out to aid navigation along trade routes by converting the globe into a flat map. Known as the Mercator projection, this method has been used for more than 400 years to create navigation charts, school maps and even Google maps.

Born Gerard De Kremer in the small river port of Rupelmonde, near Antwerp, he adopted the Latin name Mercator. A skilled engraver and mathematician, he designed inexpensive globes and created his first world map at the age of 25.

His career was brutally interrupted during the religious troubles when he was imprisoned for heresy. After his release, Mercator spent eight years in Leuven. He finally fled the Low Countries and settled in the more tolerant Duisburg, where he created his famous world map based on the Mercator projection.

But there is a problem with Mercator's map. It placed Germany at the centre of the world, exaggerated the size of Europe and North America, and shrunk Africa and South America. Several modern map-makers have developed alternatives to Mercator, although the 1569 projection is still the world's most popular map.

The Mercatormuseum in Sint-Niklaas displays several Mercator globes as well as a number of Mercator maps. The maps have helped people navigate the planet for more than four hundred years. Without Mercator, we'd all be lost.

Utopia Aalst
Utopia 1
Aalst
+32 (0)53 72 38 51
utopia.aalst.be

UTOPIA

The idea of Utopia emerged in the early 16th century in northern Belgium. Thomas More began writing his little book *Utopia* in 1515 while he was in Bruges as part of a delegation negotiating a trade deal. When talks broke down, More took the opportunity to visit his friends Hieronymus van Busleyden in Mechelen and Pieter Gillis in Antwerp. The first edition of *Utopia* was printed the following year in Leuven by the Aalst printer Dirk Martens.

When a new public library was built in Aalst, the city decided to name it 'Utopia'. Designed by Dutch Kaan Architecten, the striking modern building opened in 2018. It incorporates a large neon map of Utopia based on an illustration in Dirk Martens' first edition, along with a replica printing press and other reminders of Thomas More's radical book.

ICONIC | *ideas & inventions*

THE LANGUAGE BORDER

You can't see it. There are no border guards. No passport control. But an invisible border runs across Belgium from east to west, dividing Dutch-speaking Flanders in the north from French-speaking Wallonia in the south. (There is also a small German-speaking community in the east known as the *Ostkantone*.)

Marked out in 1961-62, the language border became law in 1963. But the border had been around for about two thousand years, ever since the Romans occupied this area of Europe.

The Romans brought Latin to the region but, when the Empire began to fall apart, Frankish tribes invaded from the east. They spoke a different language, a version of German. The Franks mainly occupied the flat land to the north, while the Latin speakers retreated to the forested uplands to the south. The language border began to take shape along the line where the hills begin, just south of Brussels. They spoke Dutch to the north, French to the south. And a mix of the two along the border.

It stayed that way until the French invaded Belgium in 1794. They introduced French to the schools and town halls of the north. Even the existing street names were changed into French. The Rozenhoedkaai in Bruges became the Quai des Rosiers. A street in Ghent called Ham was renamed Rue du Jambon.

Under the Belgian constitution of 1831, French was the official language of government. But the Dutch speakers in the north fought for the right to have their language recognised in their region. And in 1952, two Belgian researchers – one French speaker and one Dutch speaker – started to mark out a border between the two language zones. They visited every village and every farm along the invisible frontier to find out what language was spoken most widely. Ten years later, in 1963, the country agreed on a border, with Brussels given the official status of a bilingual enclave within Flanders.

There were violent protests sparked off by language rights in the 1960s and 1970s, but Belgium has changed, and language no longer dominates the country's politics.

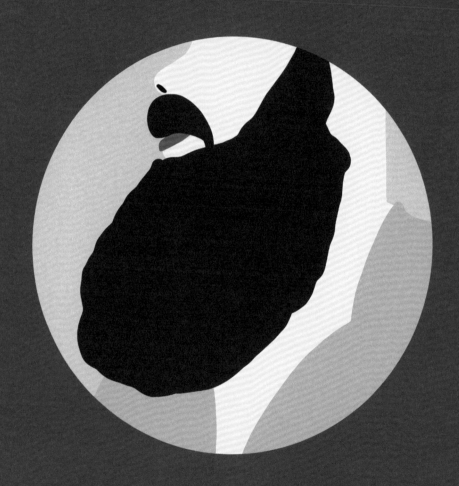

NO GOVERNMENT

It made no sense. Following elections in 2010, Belgium was without a government for 541 days. It was the longest period a democratic country had survived without a government. But the odd thing was that the country seemed to function perfectly well without anyone in charge.

The problem was a hard one to fix. The country has become deeply divided between rich, conservative Flanders in the north and poor, socialist Wallonia in the south. Maybe it could be fixed if there wasn't also a language divide running across the country.

The same problem returned following elections of 26 May 2019. The country entered another long period without a government. It has become almost impossible to form a national government after elections. But this doesn't matter too much, because most of the everyday responsibilities of government are exercised by the regions or even the local communes. It means Belgians can be quite relaxed about the lack of a federal government.

During the 2010-11 crisis, women protested by refusing to have sex, men stopped shaving, and free fries and beer were handed out to mark the day when Belgium smashed the world record for government-free days. It was an absurd situation.

The different political parties finally reached an agreement in 2011, and again in 2020, this time following 493 days of negotiations. It takes time, but a new government is always formed in the end.

Ceci n'est pas

ICONIC
expressions

Ceci n'est pas

CECI N'EST PAS

René Magritte sparked off an intense debate in 1929 when he painted a picture of a brown pipe with the caption *'Ceci n'est pas une pipe'* (This is not a pipe). The mysterious painting, which now hangs in the Los Angeles County Museum of Art (LACMA), was titled *La trahison des images* (The Treachery of Images).

The pipe became one of the most famous icons of modern art. Magritte eventually got tired of answering questions about its deep meaning. "It's just a picture," he said, "you can't stuff my pipe."

Yet the title continues to influence the way Belgians think about things. You will often come across signs that say *Ceci n'est pas* something. A door. A museum. A book. A local tour guide offers a walking tour of Brussels called 'Ceci n'est pas Bruxelles'.

When the city of Brussels invited residents in 2018 to come up with street names for the new Tour & Taxis district, they received some quirky suggestions, including Passage de la Frite (Fries Alley) and Chemin du Bonheur (Happiness Road). But maybe the strangest proposal was: Ceci n'est pas une rue. This is not a street.

It made sense, at least to a Belgian.

V-SIGN

The name Victor de Laveleye might not mean anything to most people. But he is something of a war hero in Belgium. A Brussels lawyer and local councillor, he was a great tennis player in his youth and participated in the Olympic Games of 1920 and 1924. When the German army invaded in 1940, he moved to London where he began working as a radio announcer for the BBC's Radio Belgique service.

In a radio speech on 14 January 1941, he called on Belgians to use the letter V as a symbol of resistance. He chose V as it was the first letter of *victoire* (victory) in French and *vrijheid* (freedom) in Dutch (and, conveniently, the first letter of Victor's own name). Within a few weeks, V's started to appear in chalk on walls in Belgium, the Netherlands and North France as a symbol of resistance.

Encouraged by the success, the BBC launched a 'V for Victory' campaign. By July 1941, the V-sign had spread across occupied Europe, leading to Winston Churchill's defiant gesture (often with a cigar between the raised fingers).

The V-sign was later adopted by President Eisenhower, who would raise both arms while making the V-sign. President Nixon sometimes used it to symbolise victory in the Vietnam War, but then the anti-war movement took it over in the 1960s to symbolise peace.

The V-sign has been used by the Beatles, the Solidarity movement in Poland, the Iranian Green Revolution and the Flemish nationalist party. It also turns up in millions of selfie photos in Japan, China and South Korea.

But it all started with a BBC radio broadcast by a forgotten Belgian.

NON PEUT-ÊTRE

"Yes we can," an American president once said. "No we can't, or maybe we can," might be the Belgian response. *"Non peut-être"*, in French.

The expression has become a catch phrase. No, but maybe. It is the name of a Belgian beer, a blog, a line of T-shirts and a Brussels restaurant.

It might be a better motto for Belgium than the official one, *'L'Union fait la force'* – Unity makes us stronger, which doesn't make any sense in a country that is so deeply divided.

The negative *'Non peut-être'* might seem a little odd in a progressive, modern country that hosts the European Union, NATO and several thousand multinational companies. But Belgium has been invaded and occupied many times in its history. It's only natural that people are reluctant to let others boss them around. And so they tend to be a little stubborn. "It's impossible," they will say. But then, after a pause, they correct themselves. "But maybe."

"No we can."

IK HOU VAN U /
JE T'AIME, TU SAIS

When a Belgian radio station asked listeners to choose the best Belgian song ever, they came up with an unexpected result. Not Brel singing *Ne me quitte pas*. Not Hooverphonic's *Mad About You*. But *Ik hou van u / Je t'aime, tu sais* (I love you).

This hypnotic summer waltz was originally sung in Dutch by the band Noordkaap in the 1995 film *Manneken Pis*. The film poster reflected the fairy-tale mood of the plot with its image of two glittering gold lamé shoes. The love song at the heart of the film was subsequently translated into French and recorded in a bilingual version to mark the 175th anniversary of Belgian independence. Performed by Flemish singer Stijn Meuris of Monza and Congolese-Belgian singer Marie Daulne of Zap Mama, the song was broadcast simultaneously in 12 different Belgian cities. Led by choreographer Anne Teresa de Keersmaeker, local people danced to the music in main squares across the country.

The song has been performed by many Belgian artists. Axelle Red has done a version. Scala & Kolacny Brothers covered it in 2002. It is sung at weddings, beach festivals, *fêtes de villages*. In 2013, it was performed in front of the royal family at the National Ball.

It has almost become a national anthem for this strange and divided country that always seems to be about to fall apart.

I love you, Belgium, you might want to say.

100 *Belgian Icons*

Editing and composing Derek Blyth
Illustrations Emma Verhagen
Graphic design Sarah Schrauwen

D/2020/12.005/6
ISBN 9789460582738
NUR 521, 370

© 2020, Luster Publishing, Antwerp
www.lusterweb.com – *www.curiousbelgium.com*
info@lusterweb.com

Copyright
p.62 Tintin © Hergé/Moulinsart – année en cours
p.136 Expo 58 © Fonds Lucien De Roeck 2020, *www.lucienderoeck.be*
p.144 Magritte © Succession René Magritte – Sabam Belgium 2020
p.152 Atomium © 2020 – *www.atomium.be* – SOFAM

Luster has made every effort to list all copyright holders and to obtain permission
for all illustrations according to the copyright law. Interested parties are, however,
requested to contact the publisher: *info@lusterweb.com*.

Printed in Italy by Printer Trento